PRAISE FOR
HOW TO NEGOTIATE

'*How to Negotiate* landed in my inbox during a week where I was up to my neck in negotiations. I was negotiating a major investment deal for my fledgling start-up, contractual arrangements for new clients and the acrimonious exit of a poor performing contractor. Like many I am not a natural negotiator. However, according to this book, there are things that we can all do to get better and set ourselves up for success. Mike Clayton takes you through not only *how* to negotiate but *why* negotiate, the emotions that make negotiating challenging for those of us that are not full-time negotiators, and how best to overcome these through creating the right mindset and adopting principles to remove any innate doubts. This book is a must-read for any middle-leader, entrepreneur or project professional.'
Nicola Benjamin, Founder and CEO, Project Management Global

'Another fantastic book from Mike Clayton. The content is pitched perfectly for business professionals and managers to become better negotiators, and the book is full of easy-to-remember models and hacks to boost your negotiation game. A wonderful reminder that no matter your role or rank, we all have to be good negotiators to be successful. I have given a copy of the book to each member of our team as we would all like to improve our negotiation dance moves!'
Paul Lewis, Managing Director, Pitman Training Group

THE **CREATING SUCCESS** SERIES
Over 1.8 million copies sold

ABOUT THE AUTHOR

Mike Clayton has had a long career as a project manager, consultant, educator and writer. Formerly a senior manager at Deloitte, he has trained tens of thousands of managers. Now he writes, speaks and makes videos about project and business management. His many management books cover project management, communication and personal effectiveness.

How to Negotiate

Practical and proven skills to help you get the results you want

Mike Clayton

KoganPage

First published in Great Britain and the United States in 2025 by Kogan Page Limited

Kogan Page
Kogan Page Ltd, 2nd Floor, 45 Gee Street, London EC1V 3RS, United Kingdom
Kogan Page Inc, 8 W 38th Street, Suite 902, New York, NY 10018, USA
www.koganpage.com

EU Representative (GPSR)
Authorised Rep Compliance Ltd, Ground Floor, 71 Baggot Street Lower, Dublin D02 P593, Ireland
www.arccompliance.com

Kogan Page books are printed on paper from sustainable forests.

ISBNs
Hardback   978 1 3986 2093 3
Paperback   978 1 3986 2092 6
Ebook   978 1 3986 2094 0

British Library Cataloguing-in-Publication Data
A CIP record for this book is available from the British Library.

Library of Congress Control Number
2025932689

Typeset by Hong Kong FIVE Workshop
Print production managed by Jellyfish
Printed and bound by CPI Group (UK) Ltd, Croydon CR0 4YY

CONTENTS

Introduction

Are you a negotiator?

Most people who read this question will answer 'no'. Yet everybody negotiates – often many times a day. That includes you. We negotiate at home, with our families, out and about with our friends, and at work, with our colleagues, customers, suppliers and collaborators. In a very real sense, life is a series of negotiations.

If you are a professional negotiator, whose job is negotiating large transactions, international treaties or insurance settlements, then you are one of the few people for whom I did not write this book.

Instead, it is for the vast majority of supervisors, managers, leaders and business professionals who need to negotiate as part of their day-to-day work. It offers practical advice on the essential business skill of negotiating.

The book is in three parts. Most of the first half covers the basics of negotiation, which I divide into a simple five-step process. Most of the second half gives you the tools and mental models to bring this to life and make it work for you in a wide range of situations. The final short part is about reviewing: the need to review your negotiations and a review of this book. To cap it all you will find eight helpful appendices filled with checklists, templates and a glossary with over 50 negotiating terms and acronyms.

This is the introduction to how to negotiate that you need.
Good luck!

Part 1
Negotiation basics

01
Attitude

'Attitude is everything' (nearly)

This chapter acts as an introduction to the topic of negotiation. It starts with who this book is for, what negotiation is and why it is important to you. But we know that many people – possibly you – find negotiation difficult. There are many reasons why this may be, but my message is that you don't need to.

I'll tell you the truth about negotiation and the different approaches you could take. But I shan't sit on the fence. There is one approach that I will argue is right. And if you take it, not only will you get better results, it will feel more comfortable and, crucially, enhance your professional reputation.

The negotiating context: who this book is for

Before we start, we need to understand what negotiation is. One dictionary tells me that negotiation is reaching agreement through discussion and compromise. This is not a bad description, and different dictionaries give different, but similar, results.

But this is not a great definition. 'When I use a word, it means just what I choose it to mean,' says Humpty Dumpty in Lewis Carroll's *Through the Looking Glass*. We should choose meanings that fit the context. So, before I offer the definition of negotiation we'll use in this book, let's talk about context, and who this book is for.

I have written this book to offer practical advice on the essential business skill of negotiating. It is mainly for mid-career professionals who need to negotiate as part of their day-to-day work.

It is equally important to state who this book is not for. It is not for professional negotiators, whose job is to negotiate large commercial transactions. For them, this book is light revision of the basics. I doubt they'll find anything here to take exception to. But it will lack the nuance and advanced techniques they need to negotiate at their level.

It is also not for salespeople, whose job is to negotiate transactions. And neither is it for international negotiators, setting out to broker treaties between nations.

What is negotiation?

The definition I'll use in this book is this:

Negotiation is the process of searching for an agreement that satisfies all parties.

This definition has four important components:

1 Process
This means that, if you follow the steps in that process, you will get a predictable result. This doesn't mean you will always get the outcome that you want. But it does mean that you will either find an agreement that satisfies all parties, or recognize that doing so is not, at this time, possible.

2 Searching
It takes work to achieve the agreement you and the other parties will be satisfied with. The process of getting there is one of exploration and discovery.

3 Agreement
Reaching a point where you know what will satisfy everyone is not enough. You have also to secure an agreement that will stick. This is a vital step in the process.

4 Satisfies all parties

If one or more parties are not happy with the position you reach, any agreement that you make will either unravel or cause long-term resentments. Negotiation must aim to produce something that is both fair for all sides and seen to be fair by all sides.

Why we need negotiation

Before I tell you why I think you need to negotiate, try a short exercise.

> ## Exercise
>
> Think about a typical week at work. What are the different types of negotiation you take part in? Consider every time you need to look for an agreement that satisfies you and someone else.

If I am right – and if you lead people in a professional capacity – you will find yourself negotiating all the time. Or, at the very least, several times a day. And then, of course, you'll probably go home and spend time with family or friends – and end up negotiating with them too.

But, back to your work. Negotiation is a core professional skill. It is an essential part of your job to negotiate with:

- colleagues – over role allocations, schedules and priorities;
- suppliers and business partners – over prices, delivery and deadlines;
- customers and clients – over service standards, options and complaints;
- managers and bosses – over job requirements, career progression and remuneration

To a large degree, your career success depends on your ability to negotiate.

Why we find negotiation difficult

One of the things I have noticed is that a lot of business professionals have no trouble negotiating, until someone points out to them that this is what they are doing. Because we negotiate all the time, we often fail to notice it.

But, as soon as people realize that 'I need to negotiate', they can become nervous and their confidence leaks away. Why is this?

Exercise

Do you find negotiating a challenge? If you do, why is this? What are your feelings, beliefs and assumptions about negotiation? And what makes it seem difficult to you?

For many people, negotiation seems to go against their cultural experiences. Unless you come from a culture where bargaining over prices is common, negotiation can seem alien to you. And most people aren't taught it.

Of course, small children negotiate all the time, without compunction. But, somewhere along the line, we gain inhibitions and there is nothing in our formal education that teaches us processes, strategies or techniques that we can use. We're too busy learning maths, languages, history and science for the syllabus to fit in valuable life and workplace skills like project management, influence and negotiation.

I think, at the heart of our fear of negotiation is a dilemma. We don't want people to see us as pushy. But equally, we don't want to feel that they are pushing us about.

What is driving this, however, is a misconception. It is easy to think of negotiation as a process where one person wins and the other loses. Indeed, sports lead us to think that one person winning necessarily means the other loses.

The truth about negotiation

This win-lose dynamic is not what negotiation is about. It's about finding a deal that satisfies both of you. Negotiation is about finding something that is fair.

This makes negotiation an honourable activity that we can pursue with integrity; because negotiation is about trying to produce something that is fair for all sides, you don't need to feel bad about it.

This still leaves the problem of not feeling you have the skills to negotiate. That is where this book comes in. If there are people who can negotiate well, then they must have skills, processes and techniques that are working for them. And these are the skills, processes and techniques I have documented in this book. I have stuck to the basics because, unless you take a particular interest in negotiating, these will give you what you need.

The 80:20 effect (also called the Pareto Principle) applies here. There are a great number of advanced books and academic studies about the finer points of negotiation. But the central 20 per cent of knowledge and techniques will serve you well in the vast majority (80 per cent, say) of common workplace situations.

Approaches to negotiating

Once you have a 'can do' attitude of knowing that negotiation is something you can do and that you can do it with integrity, it's time to focus on another aspect of attitude. What will be your basic approach to negotiation?

> **Exercise**
>
> Think about different times you have either negotiated or
> observed a negotiation. This can be in real life, or in a film or TV
> show. What different approaches have you seen? How would
> you characterize them?

There are four principal approaches to negotiation. These arise
from a mindset that can be:

- Your default way of approaching things. Mindsets can become
  habits that are hard to shake.

- An unconscious response to the situation, triggered by your
  emotional state at the start of, or during, a negotiation. You can
  start off one way and find your approach shifting without you
  realizing it.

- A deliberate choice, based on the outcome that you want for the
  negotiation and the relationship with the other party.

It should be obvious which of these is best. Self-control is, perhaps,
the most important single skill in a professional career. It is
certainly essential for successful negotiation.

So, if you can control your approach, what are the four choices
you have?

> ## The four negotiation approaches
>
> ### Aggressive negotiation
>
> Aggressive negotiators are highly competitive and put their own
> needs ahead those of other people. We can recognize it in
> negotiators who:

- demand, rather than ask
- are afraid to ask for help
- blame other people for setbacks
- are arrogant, intolerant, controlling or even abusive

Aggressive negotiators need to win at all costs.

Passive negotiation

Passive negotiators are prepared to place their own legitimate wants and needs below those of other people. We can recognize it in negotiators who:

- are afraid to disagree or risk rejection
- feel guilty about saying no
- aim to conciliate whenever the other person disagrees
- readily accommodate even unreasonable requests
- appear apologetic, submissive or even helpless

Passive negotiators try to prevent confrontation at all costs.

Passive-aggressive negotiation

Passive-aggressive negotiators aim to manipulate the other person. Often this means making others feel bad about pursuing their reasonable objectives. This often happens in an indirect way, so the perpetrator can persuade themselves that it's not their fault. We can recognize it in negotiators who:

- are hostile, pessimistic, cynical or even bitter
- are manipulative, deceitful or outright lie
- use sarcasm or belittle other people
- complain and adopt a victim mentality, portraying others as persecutors
- blame other people, arguing that setbacks are 'not my fault'
- disengage when things are not going well, often becoming resentful and holding a grudge

Passive-aggressive negotiators manipulate the situation to win while trying to appear a victim.

Assertive negotiation

Assertive negotiators aim to treat the other parties with respect, while standing up for what they need. We can recognize it in negotiators who:

- are confident, collaborative and direct
- say what they think and feel
- listen carefully and consider their responses
- own up to their mistakes and accept responsibility
- prioritize fairness and equity
- celebrate success

Assertive negotiators focus on getting the best outcome available.

We can think about the four approaches to negotiation in terms of a single concept: **respect**.

- Assertive negotiators show equal respect for both sides of the negotiation.
- Aggressive negotiators show little or no respect for the other party.
- Passive negotiators have less respect for themselves than for the other party.
- Passive-aggressive negotiators respect no one – not the other person nor themselves – but pretend to be respectful of the other party. The essence of this manipulative approach is that it is aggression in disguise.

For the avoidance of all possible doubt, I believe that assertive negotiation is the right attitude – and the only one that is sustainable in the long term. This is not to say that you cannot adopt a more competitive or submissive strategy within your bargaining. But if you do, you must always maintain complete respect for yourself and the other party.

Two strategies of assertive negotiation

There are two basic ways we can use an assertive approach to negotiation.

The first way is to work hard to create the best deal for both parties. This builds the relationship, based on a mindset of, 'What can I add that will match what you can add?' Here, both parties are committing to get more from the negotiation by working together collaboratively.

The second way to be equally respectful is useful when there is not enough reason to work hard to optimize the agreement. But you still want a fair deal that is equally respectful of both parties. A compromise is what you want. In a compromise, we ask, 'What will you give up, to compensate for what I'll give up?' Compromise leads to each party losing an equal amount.

Collaborative mindset

Respectful negotiation that honours the principle of integrity should never be adversarial. Confrontation, manipulation and abuse are never warranted, least of all in a professional setting. But equally, it is perfectly reasonable for you to try to get what you need from the agreement. And if you cannot, you have a right to walk away and not form an agreement. If you do so politely and respectfully, there is no need to damage the long-term relationship.

If you can balance the two priorities of respect for yourself and the needs of your 'side' with the legitimate needs of the other party, you can avoid a win-lose mindset that results in a zero-sum game.

> ## Zero-sum game
>
> A zero-sum game is one where whatever one player gains, the other player loses an equal amount. The total of the sum won and the sum lost always equals zero. Betting a pound on the toss of a coin is a zero-sum game. Both players stake a pound, so the total at stake is £2. Whoever wins keeps their pound and wins the other player's pound.
>
> Collaboration leads to an outcome where the sum is greater than zero. Compromise leads to a sum that is less than zero but, critically, with the losses shared fairly.

If both parties are prepared to work together collaboratively, they can develop creative solutions that result in both parties gaining more from the agreement than they put into it. Collaborative negotiation is not a zero-sum game. It leads to a win-win outcome.

Integrity in negotiation

Negotiation is a part of your job. It's a professional skill that you will develop and use throughout your career. So, the way you conduct each negotiation will reflect on you and your professional persona. If the way you negotiate causes people to lose trust in you, the impact on your professional reputation can be profound and long-lasting.

The conclusion is simple. You must consider the impact of every negotiation on the trust of the people around you. This means negotiating with:

- credibility and professionalism, by preparing well;
- respect for the other party to avoid the appearance of acting out of self-interest;
- commitment to doing what you promise to do;

and, above all

- being scrupulously honest and demonstrating complete integrity.

You cannot succeed in negotiating without the trust of the other party. Having integrity means that their trust in you is well placed.

Summary points

- This book is for business professionals who need to negotiate as part of their day-to-day work.
- Negotiation is the process of searching for an agreement that satisfies all parties.
- To a large degree, your career success depends on your ability to negotiate.
- Negotiation is not about win-lose but about finding a fair result.
- There are four approaches to negotiation: aggressive, passive, passive-aggressive and assertive. However, this book only recommends assertive negotiation.
- Assertive negotiation can pursue a strategy of collaboration or compromise.
- One thing matters above all: maintaining trust throughout your professional career. This means always acting with integrity.

02
Process

Trust the process

The core of this book is my five-step process for negotiating. All the advice, tips and tactics around this core will improve the results you get. But it is these five steps that will give you the confidence and capability to negotiate. Once you have them committed to you management muscle memory, every time you use them, you'll be ready to learn more and sharpen your technique.

What matters

In the opening chapter, we saw two things. First, that negotiation is part of your job. But secondly, that many of us find it uncomfortable, unfamiliar and challenging. Put simply, many people don't like negotiating.

But there are many things we do in our work that we don't enjoy. This does not make them bad or inappropriate. We can – and, I argued, you should – always negotiate with integrity. This leads to important things in your professional life, like your reputation, the trust you earn from the people you work with, and the nature of the person you see in the mirror at the start and end of every day.

A sound process can guide you along a straight path.

The other thing that matters, as well as integrity, is the outcome you can achieve from your negotiations. Notice I used the word 'negotiations' rather than negotiation. You may well not get the optimum outcome from this negotiation or that one. Indeed, it would be unlikely that you could optimize your results for every negotiation.

But consider all the negotiations you enter into, in each part of your professional life. What is their collective outcome? This is what matters. Matches are divided into games, quarters, halves and sets. And a championship is made up of many games. Your career will be made up of many negotiations.

Get the best result you can from each. Learn from every experience. And optimize your total outcome.

Trust the process

We defined negotiation as 'The process of searching for an agreement that satisfies all parties'.

The good thing about processes is that, when you follow them, you don't need to think about *what* to do next. This leaves you free to concentrate on *how* to do it, to get the best results. We can lose any anxiety about not knowing what to do.

Another benefit of a good process is predictability; when you follow the process properly, you *will* get to the end. This doesn't mean that you can predict the result. But it does mean that you have a consistent mechanism to get to the best result possible.

A good process will give you confidence in your capabilities. It therefore removes some of the resistance to starting a negotiation. And confidence is something that all negotiators need.

But here's the thing. The process for negotiation is simple, as we'll see, but there can be many hazards and pitfalls along the way. These setbacks do not mean you are doing the wrong things – or that your negotiation will fail. They are just a part of the journey. Trust the process, stay resilient and keep going.

The five-step process

A process is a series of actions that move you from a starting point to an end point or goal. And the process for negotiation is a particularly simple one. I'll describe it in five steps, and Chapters 3 to 7 will go into each of these steps in detail:

1 Step one: Prepare
   We'll look at the outcomes you want and your negotiating assets, as well as researching the other party's position. The key output will be your negotiating plan.

2 Step two: Open
   This step covers the first stage of your engagement with the other party, and we'll see that there are six things to cover when you open a negotiation.

3 Step three: Bargain
   This is where the active search for agreement happens, and the step continues until you find that agreement. This is what many people think of as 'negotiating'.

4 Step four: Close
   Finding agreement is not enough. Both parties have to state their agreement in some formal way, and achieving that is the goal of this step.

5 Step 5: Follow-up
   It could be argued that negotiation only has four steps and that this one, follow-up, is what happens *after* the negotiation process. But it is critical to understand that, if you don't do the follow-up diligently, you will undo all the hard work of steps 1 to 4. Follow-up is an essential part of the process.

Figure 2.1   Negotiating process

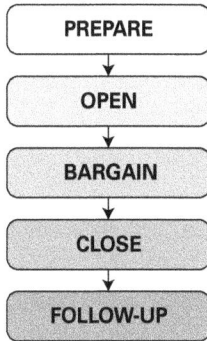

```
┌─────────────────┐
│     PREPARE      │
└─────────────────┘
         ↓
┌─────────────────┐
│      OPEN        │
└─────────────────┘
         ↓
┌─────────────────┐
│     BARGAIN      │
└─────────────────┘
         ↓
┌─────────────────┐
│      CLOSE       │
└─────────────────┘
         ↓
┌─────────────────┐
│    FOLLOW-UP     │
└─────────────────┘
```

Top tip

Until you have this process committed to your long-term memory, jot it in the back of your notebook, or keep it as a simple note on your phone, tablet or laptop. This way you can refresh your memory when you need it. You can also add extra notes from the tips that you find most useful, as you read this book.

Summary points

- The two most important things in negotiation are your integrity and the long-term outcomes you achieve.
- Negotiation is a five-step process.
- The five steps are: prepare, open, bargain, close and follow-up

03
Prepare

Failing to prepare is preparing to fail

Preparation is essential if you want a successful outcome to your negotiation. You have to understand the whole situation and plan how you will proceed. You need to assess your priorities, those of the other party and options that could satisfy those interests.

You also need to understand your own negotiating strengths and weaknesses, and use all of these to come up with a plan. This chapter starts with your own position. Then we'll look at the other party's position. Finally, we'll finish by looking at the plan you'll make for the negotiation.

Your outcomes

'What do you want from the negotiation?' The answer to this is your goal. And we usually think that this is what really matters. It is not.

What matters more is the answer to the question, 'What will you get when you've got it [your goal]?' because the answer to this is the outcome of the negotiation. And this is the change that your agreement will bring about. You may have a new contract for the supply of materials, a new roster for your team's duties or an improved remuneration package.

In Stephen Covey's best-selling book, *The 7 Habits of Highly Effective People*, habit number two is great advice for preparing to negotiate:

Begin with the end in mind.

Your negotiation goal should flow from this. What is the ideal agreement that will get you the outcome you want? This is your goal.

Write the SMARTEST goals you can

A familiar framework for writing effective goals is the SMART framework. There are many variants. For setting negotiating goals, this version is, perhaps, the smartest!

- **Specific:** Be as clear and precise as you can, which can take a lot of work. A part of this is to add numerical measures where possible.

- **Meaningful:** Set a goal that can produce a meaningful and worthwhile outcome. There is no point in negotiating over something trivial that you can get in a simpler way.

- **Ambitious:** Choose a goal that will stretch your negotiating skills. You want the best result that you can possibly get, but it must also be...

- **Realistic:** Avoid a degree of ambition that will waste your time and that of the other party. Remember that the other party will need to be satisfied by your agreement too.

- **Trimmable**: Have fall-back positions in case you cannot achieve your ambitious goal.

- **Ethical:** Achieving your goal must be through ethical means and produce a responsible outcome.

- **Substantiated:** Do your homework to make sure you have evidence to support your assessments of what's available and how much you might expect to pay for it.

- **Timeframes:** There are two aspects to think about: first, the timeframe within which you want to negotiate; second, is the timeframe over which the agreement is likely to extend. Are you looking for a short one-off transaction or a long-lasting relationship that can continue for years?

Your position

When you know what your ideal outcome is, the next thing to think about is your minimum acceptable outcome. This is commonly known as your 'bottom line'.

A 'negotiating position' is the set of things you want from the negotiation and the limit you set on what you will offer in return. However, when we come to look at 'their position', it is important to recognize that when the other party states a position, you should never take it at face value.

There are various forms of a negotiating position:

1 your real position, which you will never disclose

2 your opening position, which you state at the outset of the negotiation

3 your stated position at various stages as the negotiation progresses

The same will be true of the other party. Inexperienced negotiators too often take the positions of the other side at face value and don't probe with questions or challenge it sufficiently.

In developing your position, you need to figure out where you must stop negotiating and walk away. So, your bottom line is also known as your walk-away point. But how do you know where this lies?

The best answer to this question was developed by Roger Fisher and William Ury of the Harvard Negotiation Project. In their classic book on negotiation, *Getting to Yes*, they described the BATNA.

Your BATNA

Never just pick an arbitrary limit to act as your bottom line. And certainly don't choose a walk-away point based on an emotional assessment of the value you want to achieve. You can only properly assess your bottom line if you know your BATNA.

Your BATNA is your *best alternative to a negotiated agreement.*

Figure out what you could do if the negotiation fails. Then consider the value of your best option. If your negotiation cannot reach an agreement that gives you more value than this, you have to stop the negotiation. If you don't, you will just be negotiating about the size of your loss. Your BATNA gives you your bottom line: your walk-away point.

Any agreement that is better than your BATNA is a success for your negotiation. But, if you don't know your BATNA, then you risk reaching an agreement that is worse for you than not agreeing. The more research you do into the alternatives available to you, the more you can develop a robust BATNA that will support you in your negotiation.

Calculating the value of your agreement

There are different ways to calculate the value of an agreement. But the two factors that go into the calculation are the same:

1 the amount you contribute to the agreement: your cost
2 the amount you get from the agreement: your benefit

From these, we most often calculate value in one of three ways:

1 Value as a net benefit: Value = Benefit – Cost
2 Value as a cost-to-benefit ratio: Value = Benefit ÷ Cost
3 Value as a return on investment: Value = (Benefit – Cost) ÷ Cost

All of these work slightly differently, and different organizations adopt different methods. Finance professionals most often use return on investment (ROI), which is the net benefit divided by the total cost.

But what if you get an offer that is below your BATNA? This doesn't mean you should get up and walk away. Chances are that this is a tactic from the other party. However, if the other party looks like they will hold to their position, and you can't raise the offer above your BATNA, you will have to walk away. At this point, you will need to tell the counterparty that this is the case.

But don't share with them your precise walk-away point. If you did, they could simply raise their offer a tiny bit above it. On the other hand, if you tell them that they are well below the point where you're going to have to walk away, they will have to think carefully about where they are in relation to their own bottom line.

Your leverage

Leverage takes its name from the mechanical advantage we get from a lever. It is the ability to apply a small force to move something heavy. It's all about a disproportionate amount of effort and outcome.

In negotiating, it refers to the advantage one party has to move the negotiation towards an agreement that favours their objectives.

However, this does not have to be a real advantage. What matters is what each party thinks, so leverage can be about a perceived advantage. You might, for example, have a big advantage but, if the other side is unaware, you don't have any leverage. On the other hand, you may not actually have an advantage at all. But if the other party thinks you do, then you have leverage.

> ## 'I'm going to make him an offer he can't refuse'
>
> We often think of leverage as referring to a substantial negotiating advantage, such as a monopoly position, privileged information or the power to compel or coerce. However, whilst these are forms of leverage, the gangster approach offers a narrow interpretation that gives little opportunity to use leverage in real life. It also invites abuses.

Leverage is a compelling advantage that can come in many different forms. Examples include:

- a unique capability or high-value proposition
- the other party's sense of fairness
- knowledge, influence or advantage
- access to resources, assets or services
- ability to wait for, defer or forego a benefit

Often it is possible to increase the leverage you have, based on how you present your advantage to the other party. Chapter 10 will go more deeply into the techniques of influence that apply to negotiation. But there is a saying in marketing that 'people buy benefits, not features'. You will have more leverage when you focus less on the features that your proposition offers to the other party, and more on the benefits they will get as a result of taking advantage of your proposition. The strongest arguments are based on value.

You may wonder why the other party's sense of fairness is a source of leverage. Human beings are wired for fairness. Most of us want others to be fair and we work to be fair ourselves. So, when you make an offer, I will feel a natural pressure to respond equitably. Yes, there are some people who don't care about fairness, and trained negotiators may be able to recognize and override this instinct. But the urge for fairness is a real phenomenon.

Your flexibility

It is a truism that negotiation is about give and take, also called reciprocity or reciprocation. So, you will need to think through the whole range of:

- benefits you can offer
- concessions you can ask for in return
- benefits they may be able to offer you
- concessions you could give in return

The more ideas you can come up with and the more flexible you can be, the more likely you are to find a beneficial agreement for both parties.

What gives this magic is that you and your counterparty may ascribe different values to different things. And these differential values are what create a successful negotiation.

Example

As an example, let's say you are close to agreeing the purchase of a new car. But you feel you don't have a good enough deal. The dealer, however, knows that the price you have reached is at the limit of what they can offer and retain their minimum margin on the sale. What is the flexibility?

Here are some examples:

- You, the buyer, could ask the dealer to include some low-value accessories, like floor mats and a pack of car care products. The retail cost of these is high (often deliberately so) but the cost to the dealer is low.

- The dealer could offer you a discounted five-year service agreement. You get a benefit from the discount, and it gives the dealer a guaranteed income stream and the potential for further income from added services outside the agreement.

- The dealer may have a quota to meet for sales in the quarter. If you continue the negotiation towards the end of the quarter, your leverage increases. Here, time has a greater value to the dealer than to you.

Yourself

Assessing your own strengths and weaknesses will become less necessary the more experienced you become with negotiation. But, early in your negotiating career, as you seek to develop your skills, this is a valuable exercise. It's also valuable as a part of your preparation for any negotiation that stands out as particularly large, complex or important, in comparison to your previous experience.

Undertake a self-audit. Carefully assess:

- the strengths you bring to the negotiating process: your experience, skills, knowledge and values;
- the weaknesses and vulnerabilities you could have in this negotiation;
- what you have learned from previous experience of negotiating that you can deploy in the next one.

Research

Who will you be negotiating with? What do you know about them and their position? It may be a colleague you work with every day. In this instance, you won't need to do much active research. But, on the other hand, it may be a new contractor who is pitching to support you in a project you are leading.

It has never been easier to do some basic research on organizations and people. If you go into a meeting without knowing the basics of the organization with whose representatives you are negotiating, you are not doing your job. What can you find out about them?

Split your research into the organization and the people. Anything you learn could prove valuable and may be a source of flexibility or even leverage.

Organizational research checklist

Here is a list of things to research about the organization you will be negotiating with:

- Previous relationship and negotiations with your organization.
- Base information from their website and social media channels.
- Range of products and services.
- Key personnel at senior level and in the part of the organization you are dealing with.
- Whether they have been in the news or if there have been any big changes recently.
- Who their competitors, suppliers and customers are.
- Who else they might be negotiating with at the same time.
- The culture of the organization – and any internal politics, if you can find out.
- What is motivating them in this negotiation and what they need from it.
- What they want or need, that you may have or be able to offer.
- Are there any potential ethical concerns?

Produce a briefing sheet that will put key facts and data ready to hand.

Individual research checklist

Here is a list of things to research about an individual you will be negotiating with, whom you don't already know:

- What can colleagues tell you about this person?
- What can you learn from professional social media channels? LinkedIn is excellent for this.
- What other presence do they have on the web?
- What is motivating them in this negotiation?
- What do they need from it?
- What do they want from it?
- What do they fear from it?

If you will be negotiating with more than one person, you will need to repeat your research for each, but add to your research:

- What are the relationships within the team?
- What are the alliances and tensions between people?
- Is there a formal hierarchy?
- What are the patterns of influence outside the hierarchy?
- How might these dynamics affect the way they negotiate?
- Who do you most need to influence?
- And who is really in charge? (This may not be the same as the person above.)
- How can you turn this to your advantage?

Produce a briefing sheet that will put key facts and data ready to hand.

Often, negotiations can hinge on something very surprising – perhaps even something that is not on the agenda for discussion. Humans conduct negotiations, so our unconscious desires and fears can get in the way of making a rational decision. Sometimes, to conclude the negotiation and reach agreement, you will need to discover their blockers, get them into the open and find a way around them.

REAL-WORLD EXAMPLE   Protective boss

A colleague tells the story of negotiating the sale of a new accounting system with a finance director. He had done everything right, encouraging the potential buyer to articulate every possible objection. No objections remained, yet his prospective client would still not commit.

My colleague felt there was nothing wrong with the relationship; indeed, the feeling was strong. So he suggested: 'Let's get a coffee and go for a walk' – which they did. At some point he confessed his confusion: 'You have no objections and the system is right for your company: what's the problem?'

The answer was the finance director's senior accountant. She was nearing retirement and fearful of having to learn a new system. The FD felt that if he could delay the decision long enough, he could save her the trouble.

Like the best negotiators, my colleague found an option that benefited both. He arranged for the senior accountant to visit a reference site where she could see how easy the system was to use. She returned enthused by the potential of the new system. The FD signed the contract, and my colleague got the deal for the cost of a coffee, some phone calls and a rail ticket for the accountant.

Their position

We saw earlier that a 'negotiating position' is the set of things you must have from the negotiation and the limit you will set on what you can offer in return. Each party has its own position.

From what you have learned about the other party from your research, consider what their true position might be. You won't be able to know, so the best approach will be to come up with a range of scenarios, based on different assumptions.

For each assumption, ask yourself what things they might say or do during a negotiation that would indicate either that the assumption is false or that it is reasonable. This way, you can gradually eliminate some scenarios and underline others as remaining plausible.

Of course, their opening position will be part of their negotiating strategy: an inflated list of desires that may even exceed what they hope to get, let alone what they expect to get. But, as the negotiation goes on, there will be more statements of their position.

Inexperienced negotiators can easily fall into the trap of taking the other side's position at face value. Don't do that. Challenge it with questions about what is possible, what is important and what is really necessary. A good way to do that will be to ask the other person to explain elements of their position in greater detail. The more they say, the more clues there will be about what each component of their stated position means to them.

Options

What are the different ways you can conduct your negotiation? How could you open, what positions can you state, what concessions could you seek and what can you concede when pushed? At what stages will you try to hold out, before falling back to a lesser position, on the way to your ultimate bottom line?

You are looking for this negotiation's zone of possible agreement (ZOPA). This is where your interests overlap with theirs. We'll look at that in more detail in Chapter 13 about negotiating traps.

Negotiating plan

Your goal answers the question 'What?' and your desired outcome answers the question 'Why?' for the negotiation. These leave your plan to answer the other questions:

- When?
- Where?
- Who?
- How?
- What if?

Let's start with the when and the where. These are logistical matters, but that does not mean you should leave them to chance. Time and place can have a big impact on the psychology of the negotiation. For example, two groups of three negotiators sitting on opposite sides of a table in a small room will feel very different to the same people around a large round table in a spacious room.

Consider the relative merits of pushing for a 'home advantage' of negotiating at your own premises against conceding that advantage to the other party. Of course, you can also opt for a neutral venue, or hold the negotiation virtually, with video conferencing.

And timing is not just about the date, which can clearly impact a time-sensitive negotiation, but also the time of day. People get less tolerant as they get hungry, so a negotiation running towards lunchtime or the end of the day can become more easily heated. We also make snap decisions as a notional deadline, like lunch, approaches. And if you are negotiating across time zones, consider what will allow most participants to be there during their working day.

Next, you need to think about who should be on your negotiating team. Chapter 12 will cover teamworking in detail, so let's leave this as an open question as to who needs to be present and what specific responsibilities each team member should have.

This brings us to the how. Here is a list of things to prepare:

- your opening position
- questions you want to ask the other party
- requests you might make of them
- concessions you are prepared to offer
- an agenda for the meeting

In the appendices, you will find:

- a negotiation preparation checklist
- a one-page negotiation plan template
- a sample negotiation agenda

The last piece of your plan needs to consider contingencies. What could go wrong in the negotiation and how can you handle it? We don't do this because we believe we can properly anticipate everything that could happen. Rather, we do it to give us the confidence that we know things can go wrong, yet we can deal with them.

Identify a few sample scenarios and figure out the sorts of things you can do to stabilize the situation and prepare to move forward – or withdraw. The confidence of feeling well prepared will be a big asset for you, as a negotiator.

Summary points

- Know what you want: determine your desired outcomes and goal for your negotiation.
- Articulate an effective negotiating goal using the SMARTEST framework: Specific, Meaningful, Ambitious, Realistic, Trimmable, Ethical, Substantiated and with a Timeframe.
- Define your end position with respect to your BATNA: Best alternative to a negotiated agreement.
- Identify your points of leverage: advantages the other party will perceive you to have.

- Determine your points of flexibility to vary your offer and requests, to secure a good agreement.
- Do your research into the other party: the organization (if relevant) and the individuals.
- Try to anticipate what the other side's position might be.
- Build a negotiating plan that answers the questions when, where, who, how and what if...

04
Open
First impressions matter

You have done your preparation, and I know that you are raring to go. When you meet the other party to negotiate, it can be tempting to dive in. But don't be in too much of a rush. Before you get into trading demands and concessions, you need to set the tone.

It may be a small part of the process in terms of time, but the opening step of the negotiation process is mighty. It more than pulls its weight.

There's a reason for this that it pays to remember. Negotiation is a human process. Ultimately, it is two people, representing their sides, trying to reach an agreement that they and their people can benefit from.

The whole of this step is about those people coming to an understanding about one another, their aims, and how they are going to work together to achieve them.

A perspective on negotiation

One way to think about negotiation is as a form of polite argument:

> Negotiation is conflict, conducted respectfully, and mediated by a clear process.

The opening step of the negotiation is therefore where the parties establish that respect and agree the process they will follow.

To achieve a satisfactory start to the collaborative steps of the negotiation, the open stage must achieve six things. We'll cover these in a sequence that is most effective. But in reality, some of these will happen in parallel, then continue throughout this step and on into the bargaining stage.

It should go without saying that, where people are involved, things can vary. So, this may not always be the right sequence for you. But I will indicate the logic as we go through.

The dance: first impressions

You only get one chance to make a first impression.

My father told me this, so it must be true! First impressions are powerful because people tend to take shortcuts in our thinking. We read a situation and it forms biases in our minds that can affect our choices and behaviour for a long time.

You cannot control what people think. But you can present yourself in such a way that they are more likely to think in some ways, and less likely to think in others. Everything about the way you look and move, what you say and what you do will communicate something to the people around you. You cannot not communicate. And the people around you – especially those who are meeting you for the first time – will make judgements as a result.

The conclusion, therefore, must be that you have a choice in how you present yourself. And, like it or not, you can direct that choice. For the best results, choose an impression that communicates a strong positive impression.

To do this, you need to understand the context. This is why we research the people and the culture they come from. But whilst ritual forms of courtesy may vary from culture to culture, there will always be a value in presenting yourself respectfully and politely. There are relatively few people with the power and authority to breach conventions like these and still succeed in negotiating. Most of them are fictional characters in books and drama.

So, what is it that contributes to a positive first impression? Here's a checklist. It will not tell you the 'right' approach to take. That will depend on the context: the culture, the people, and what you are negotiating. For example, it will start with facial expression. In most contexts, a warm smile will be a good choice. But if the subject of the negotiation is sombre or the culture of the people you're meeting is reserved, this may be inappropriate.

You may also find that some of these are not as relevant in some cultures, but highly relevant in others. But, equally, unless you do your research, you may be surprised at how important a seemingly small detail can be.

First impression checklist

- Facial expression
- Eye contact
- Posture
- Position in the room
- Greeting (for example, handshake)
- Grooming
- Clothing style (formality or colour, for example)
- Standard of clothing (quality, which can be code for status)
- Clothing accessories (ties, belts or jewellery, for example)
- Business accessories (pens, notebooks or devices, for example)

To illustrate this with a stark contrast, consider these two alternatives.

First alternative: you arrive only just on time, flustered, sweaty and dishevelled. Your clothes are ill-suited to the environment you are in, and not at all the same style as those around you. Because you were in a hurry, you had a quick shower and paid little attention to your appearance. After a rushed greeting, you take your papers out of an old bag and place a scruffy bundle on the table, along with a dog-eared notepad and a chewed biro. This will create an impression.

Second alternative: you have arrived in good time and taken a moment to check your appearance in the cloakroom. As others arrive, you greet them politely, noticing that your standard and style of dress is broadly the same as theirs – perhaps half a notch above in terms of quality and formality. You spent a while this morning choosing accessories, attending to your grooming and cleaning your shoes. When you get your papers out of a well-cared-for bag, they are in a neat portfolio. Your notebook is also smart and your pen is a nice one – though not necessarily expensive. This will create an impression.

Exercise

How would you compare the impressions created in the two alternative examples? How do you think they might influence the way the other party will deal with you in the negotiation?

These two impressions are different, and they are your choice. Getting it right takes little extra effort. What you want is simple. You want the other party to think: 'Aha! This person is well pre-pared, can negotiate effectively and is someone to respect.'

The components of your first impression are about how you enter the room, how you look and act, how you greet the other people, and therefore how prepared you are for negotiation.

The dance: rapport

Now you have made a first impression, you want to start to build a relationship and win their trust. We do this with rapport. Rapport is a sense of understanding one another and feeling a bond. So, you need to take some time to get to know one another. Your negotiation is less likely to go badly, with disrespectful behaviour and even deceit, when people have got to know one another.

Professional small talk

Building and, later, developing a professional relationship needs conversation and there is a simple acronym to help you remember the topics that are suitable: FROGS:

- Friends – particularly professional friends and colleagues that you have in common.
- Relatives – as you get to know someone, you can find out about and, later, enquire about, their family.
- Organizations – that you have worked for or with.
- Geography – places you have lived and worked, or holiday destinations.
- Social interests – for many people, this is sport, but not for everyone!

A good way to allow for rapport building is to start a meeting with getting refreshments, which offers the opportunity for small talk. As you do this, make sure you listen carefully. A top tip is that people like you if you talk about topics they are interested in. So, ask them about themselves, because that will allow them to introduce subjects they care about. Pay attention to:

- what matters to them
- useful snippets of information about them
- their body language, expressions and vocal tones

Also practise empathy. Try to appreciate their point of view, so you can understand their way of thinking, which will inform how they negotiate later. You may disagree with them, and you may not even like them. But stay respectful and empathize.

By the way, if your disagreement and dislike are profound, and linked to a substantial matter like values, you may want to ask whether they are the right person or organization for you to negotiate with. Or, indeed, if you are the right person to negotiate with them. For ethical reasons, you may want to walk away from the negotiation and protect your integrity. After all, this is a workplace negotiation, not international conflict resolution!

All of this may help you later, in the bargaining stage, either because you have learned something of their position, or you can better read their unconscious signals.

Their authority to negotiate

Now you have started building a rapport, it's time to get down to business. But the last thing you want to do is invest all your time and negotiating capital in reaching an agreement, only to find that the other person says something like, 'Sorry, I can't confirm this. I need to go back to my boss.'

The reality is that, at work, we often negotiate as representatives of the decision-maker. There is nothing wrong with this. But it is important to find out as early as possible if this is the case. It is a common tactic for organizations to gain one extra concession when their counter-party thinks they have a deal. They make their 'boss' excuse and then come back, saying something like, 'My boss likes the deal, but is not prepared to sign yet. They are insisting that you also…'

It is psychologically hard not to see this last concession as a necessary step, to save the deal. In Chapter 11, we'll look at the psychology of this. It's called the sunk cost trap.

Here, all that matters is you avoid being faced by this simple negotiator's trick (sorry, tactic). So, once you have some rapport, check what authority the other party has to enter into or proceed towards an agreement. You want to be sure that, if you make an agreement with the person sitting across the table from you, that agreement will stick.

This raises the question of what to do if you discover that the person you are negotiating with is not empowered to make an agreement. There are two scenarios to consider.

The first scenario is when you have been led to expect that they would have the power and that is why you are there: you have the power to commit your organization to an agreement. This may leave a power imbalance that, in your culture, is disrespectful. You will need to find an appropriate way to pause the negotiation or withdraw from it.

As you would expect, this does not mean getting angry, throwing around insults and leaving in a spectacular display of righteous indignation. Leave that for the characters in melodramas. One tactic is to gracefully interpret this not as a snub, but as a delay. 'That's fine,' you might say, 'I am happy to wait until your boss can join us.'

The second scenario recognizes that, in most cases, this is just the way it is. Carry on with the opening step and move into bargaining as you would have done. But, during the bargaining, calibrate what you ask for, and the concessions you offer, accordingly. Remain mindful that someone is hidden behind them with a whole agenda that you may know anything about.

But let's assume all is well. If they have the authority they need, you know you can negotiate with confidence, so it's time to move on.

The basis for the meeting

You may have already had this conversation as both parties prepared for their negotiation. But, even if you have, it does no harm to confirm this in person. What is the scope of the negotiation you are about to enter? And, if it is a big negotiation that will span more than one session, what is the scope of the conversation you are about to have?

In this context, there are two elements to scope:

1 How far will you take the negotiation?
Are you aiming to come to a final agreement or just to move towards the agreement?

2 What aspects of the negotiation will you cover?
Are you working on the whole breadth of the negotiation or a narrow component of it?

With this agreed, the last element of the conversation is the process you will use to negotiate. If there is already an agenda, now is the time to review it and either confirm it or recast it, based on your conversations.

With this done, you know the process, so it's time to focus briefly on the details...

Admin and ground rules for the negotiation

Let's get admin out of the way, because nobody finds it compelling. But it is necessary to think about things like timings, record keeping, use of technology, access to office services and, for the host, indicating accessibility, resources and where restrooms and other facilities are.

In some circumstances, there may be more specialized admin arrangements, like physical security, interpretation and translation, or contingencies in the case of disruption.

Admin and ground rules merge, but ground rules are more about behaviours in the room and what is appropriate. If you are negotiating within your own organization, this may not be necessary, but with a new negotiating partner from a different culture, this is an important way to align cultural expectations and ensure neither party inadvertently gives offence.

Typical matters for negotiation ground rules

- Are some things allowed or not allowed within the meeting room?

- Commitments to mutual respect and standards of behaviour.

- Disclosure of any interests that may be relevant but not known.

- Who, on each side, is empowered to speak authoritatively?

- What's the process for requesting a timeout, stepping away or taking a break?

- For video calls, is 'camera off' acceptable?

- How are notes going to be recorded, if they are?

- Is one person going to record notes for both parties or will each party record their own notes?

- Is voice recording or AI transcription acceptable?

- How will you formalize the final agreement?

- How will you record and (if appropriate publish) what is agreed?

- Confidentiality during and after the negotiation:

  o Commitment to negotiate in good faith – this may seem obvious, but by making commitments out loud, in front of others, they create an enhanced psychological barrier to unethical behaviour.

  o How will you resolve disputes or deadlocks that arise? – this might include escalation, mediation or arbitration.

The positions

With all the interpersonal relationship building and process formalities out of the way, you are nearly ready to start bargaining. Before you do, however, you need to know where your starting point will be. This is where each party will state their opening position.

The obvious question that arises is that of who should go first. In Chapter 13, Traps, I will discuss the relative merits for a negotiator of going first or second. You will clearly want to get any advantage you can from this. However, if you have prepared well, this is unlikely to make a big difference. We'll set this aside and come back to it later.

Most often you will want to start by inviting the other party to share what they want to get from the negotiation:

- What are they hoping to achieve?
- What would they see as a good deal?
- What is their opening position?

You probably want to hear their position before you put your position on the table, because, if their outcome is more favourable to you than you expect from your preparation, you may want to revise your starting position to be more assertive.

Then, you would tell the other party what you want from the negotiation:

- what you are hoping to achieve
- what you would see as a good deal
- your opening position

You won't be alone in wanting to hear from the other side before sharing your position. So expect a little game of chicken as neither of you wants to go first! If this happens you have some options:

1 You can play the game, not back down, and hope you can place them at a disadvantage by forcing them to go first.

2 You can hope to assert your confidence by stepping forward and stating your position first.

3 You could agree to decide it by the toss of a coin.

4 You could both agree to place a written opening statement into a sealed envelope and exchange them simultaneously. Both parties could then have some reading and discussion time, before reconvening for the bargaining stage.

In a sales negotiation, there is normally an expectation that the seller will start off by putting their terms to the buyer first. They are likely to have a price or some form of schedule of rates, even if it's not published.

If the other party is the seller, then it is reasonable to ask them to state some or all their price, their conditions and their terms at the outset.

If you are the seller, you may have to concede this ground. But if you are negotiating about bespoke services or products, it is also reasonable to ask if the prospective buyer is able to give an indication of their budget.

Summary points

The six things you need to do to open a negotiation are:

1 Make a strong, positive first impression.

2 Build a rapport, and therefore a level of trust, with the person or people in the other party.

3 Establish the authority the other party has to make a binding agreement.

4 Agree with the other party the basis for the negotiation meeting.

5 Discuss and agree admin and ground rules for the negotiation.

6 Get both parties' opening positions on the table, ready for the bargaining step.

05
Bargain
The ol' give 'n' take

For many people, the bargaining step *is* negotiation, because this is the step where we negotiate. This is certainly where the action happens; the parties come together to forge a shared agreement out of many small points of acceptance and dispute.

Like many good plays and movies, the bargaining stage has a three-act structure.

Figure 5.1   Three-act bargaining structure

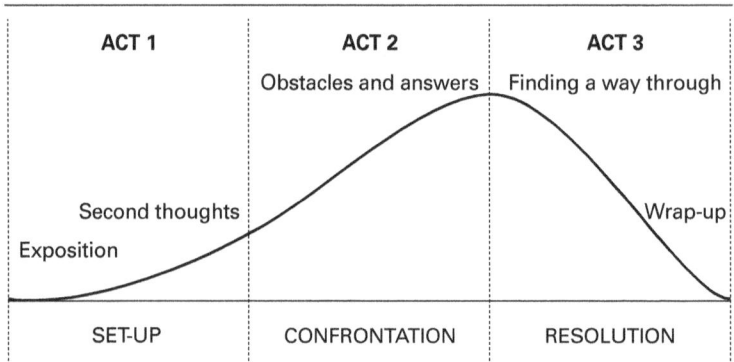

ACT 1	ACT 2	ACT 3
	Obstacles and answers	Finding a way through
Second thoughts		Wrap-up
Exposition		
SET-UP	CONFRONTATION	RESOLUTION

The first act of the bargaining step is the set-up. We enter the act with the positions on the table and our first step is to review them, understand what they mean and make a first response. When we see how things are shaping up, like any protagonist, we may have second thoughts. We will review our strategy and, ultimately, decide if we are prepared to go forward.

Of course, it is only in a drama where the hero will always answer the call to adventure. But, assuming you choose to continue, Act 2 will see a series of obstacles in your path and a constant challenge to overcome them. This is the confrontation. You can expect drama, crises and twists along the way.

If all goes well, however, you will find a way through to the resolution. Forming the final agreement will wrap up the drama... sorry, negotiation.

But wait, there is more. What about the final scene? That is the next step, closing, where the parties come together and formally close the deal. After that, what happens is the epilogue. We'll see that in the follow-up step.

Set-up: exposition

Once the opening step is complete and both parties' opening positions are clear, you can start to explore them by asking questions and listening carefully to the answers. At this stage, listening and understanding is all you should do. It is not time to respond, defend or attack. Take turns in understanding each other and clarifying your own position.

Of course, these are not final positions, but they are an indication of the direction you each want to go in – your hopes and fears. By the end of this part of Act 1, you should be able to make a good, objective assessment of the challenges ahead.

Set-up: second thoughts

Now you can make a careful review of whether it is worth proceeding: is an agreement likely to be possible? And how much work is it likely to take?

The first thing to consider is whether there is enough overlap between the needs, desires and concerns of the two parties. At one extreme, the overlap will be evident and potentially large, making a satisfying agreement easy to achieve. At the other, it may appear that there is no overlap and that agreement is not possible. You will want to test that quickly, to avoid wasting time on fruitless discussions.

Assuming that what you conclude lies between these extremes, the second thing to consider is what obstacles and sticking points you are likely to encounter. This is not to scare yourself about the difficulties that lie ahead. Rather it is to start thinking through the requests and concessions you may want to make, and about the problems you'll need to solve along the way.

Now may also be the time to review your negotiating strategy. The options you have are to:

1 **Negotiate hard.** Aim for a quick deal that optimizes your outcome, possibly at the risk of damaging the long-term relationship. This will only be appropriate where the relationship is not important to you, or an optimal outcome is a top priority.

2 **Easy concessions.** Be prepared to make multiple concessions and accept that your final outcome will be less than ideal. This is the approach you would take if optimizing the result is not critical, but maintaining and growing the relationship with the other party is. This is the principle of the 'loss leader' that retailers use to draw in new customers at the cost of minimal transaction profit, or even a loss.

3 **Walk away.** Even if you believe an agreement is possible, is it worth the effort? If you anticipate a lot of work to reach an agreement, which will then have relatively little value to you, you have to question the cost-effectiveness of the negotiation. And, if the conclusion is that the benefit does not justify the work required, then now is the time to politely withdraw from the negotiation.

4 **Compromise to get agreement.** This is likely to be your most frequent approach. You'll be trading concessions with one another until you reach a point where you both agree you have

reached an equitable position. You each feel you have gained and given enough to make for a fair trade. Compromise is often disparagingly described as the point where both parties are equally unhappy. This need not be so. Ideally, you will be equally happy.

5 **Collaborate for a win-win.** This strategy does not depend on how hard or easy it looks like it will be to achieve agreement. Instead, it is the strategy to choose where an agreement is important to both parties. And both of you want to work hard to make it as good as possible. In doing this, you will also build and enhance the relationship. This may be a wonderful by-product of the process, or it might be one of your objectives. This is the most time-consuming strategy and it will demand patience, understanding, goodwill and a lot of creativity.

Confrontation: obstacles

Act 2 of the bargaining step sees us at the dead centre of the negotiation process. And Act 2 of a drama is where all the action happens. Our protagonist must face obstacles and crises, enjoy wins and suffer setbacks. There may be a disaster or a twist to confound them, but they will usually pull through.

One thing all good negotiators know is that it is easier to build agreement on agreement. So they will start with the common ground and make as much progress as they can, early on, focusing on the easy things.

When they meet disagreement, good negotiators don't argue. They listen carefully, acknowledge what they have heard and work hard to understand the other party's point of view. Then they divide up the pie.

Top tip
Divide up the pie

It is easier to build agreement based on an agreement than it is to build agreement based on a disagreement. So, when you find something you disagree on, look for ways to divide that thing into two, three or more parts. Then note which parts you agree on. So, for example you might disagree with my valuation of a service schedule. That's a big disagreement. Can I make it into a smaller one?

In this case, I would divide the pie into three. My valuation is based on my assumptions, the methodology I used and the calculation I made. Which of those is the problem?

If, for example, it is my assumptions, we can divide those down into individual assumptions. Not only am I securing layers of agreement from you, I am also demonstrating that our disagreement is really very small (although it may, of course, be material).

We can respond to some of the objections by making and request-ing a progressive series of offers and concessions. A series of small increments is always better than making one big offer or conces-sion. It is easier to get agreement and allows you to bank a series of solutions. This gives a palpable feeling of progress and agreement, setting the tone for more agreement to come.

If your overall strategy is to compromise, each party is likely to be making concessions to one another. If, on the other hand, you are aiming for a win-win through collaboration, you will be more likely to be making offers and suggesting enhancements to the deal.

Confrontation: answers

When you know what the issues are, and what you disagree on, you can start to work on resolving each one together. You will make and receive offers. When you get an offer from the other party, always ask yourself 'how does it sound?'

It may not sound anything like good enough. But remember, it's only an offer. Your next step is to request a bigger concession or make a counteroffer. There are two main ways that you can make that counteroffer:

The first is the 'if you…, then we…' formulation:

- 'If you were to do this'
- 'If you were to accept that'
- 'If you were to commit something'

… then we would be able to do, accept or commit something else.

The second formulation is the 'if we…, would you…?' formulation:

- 'If we were to do this'
- 'If we were to offer that'
- 'If we could accept this'

'… then would you do, offer or accept this other thing?' or 'would you commit something else?'

Notice that these are all in the form of questions. This makes them sound more like an inquiry than a proposal. It allows you both to explore the counteroffer and the parameters around it.

Questions feel a lot less pushy and a lot more collaborative than a proposal, or even an offer:

- 'If we do this, we would want you to do that.'
- 'We would like you to change this. If you do, we'd be prepared to do that.'

These kinds of blunt approaches risk quickly breaking rapport. That is what can lead to a deadlock in a negotiation. The more you conduct your negotiation as a series of questions, the more open the other party will be to exploring options. And, when a positive answer emerges that both parties can agree on, you will have taken a step towards a negotiated agreement.

Top tip

Does the other party's offer sound too good to be true?

Trust your gut. If it sounds too good to be true, then it probably is. There may be a catch that you haven't spotted, or simply conditions attached that you need to better understand before you can evaluate it. You might have misinterpreted what they said.

Or it's possible that they have misspoken, in which case don't try to take advantage. Not only is that unethical, but they are likely to change their mind later, and that will create problems.

What about when you are asked for a concession? Here, your first response should be a defence, but not an outright rejection of the request. Acknowledge it and clarify if you need to. Then let them know if it's a difficult ask. Make no immediate commitment and ask for time to think about it, noting that you may not be able to offer all of it.

The reason for this is simple. When you make a concession too quickly, it feels easy to the other party and leaves them wondering whether they could have asked for more and got it. That disappointment leaves them uncomfortable and may ultimately undermine their trust in you.

By the way, this also means that, if you're asking for a concession, you should not expect the other party to say 'yes' too readily. They too will probably know that this would be foolish.

Top tip

The golden rule of concessions is that you should only make a concession when you get something of equal value to you in return.

The corollary to this is that you want to ensure that each successive concession that you make is smaller than the one before. This way you can keep the negotiation from spiralling out of control. If each concession is smaller than the last, your negotiation will converge.

Ideally, each concession should be no more than half the value of the one before. That way, you can anticipate easily where the conclusion of the concession process will end up for you.

Going into a negotiation, you should have a prepared list of concessions that you can offer, and another list of concessions that you can ask for. But of course, this doesn't mean that other things won't occur to you and your team during the negotiation. The list should not be a constraint on your thinking, but it will mean you are ready for the bargaining that will need to happen.

This smooth series of offers and counteroffers will sometimes be disrupted by something big and unexpected – sometimes known as a 'Black Swan event'. When this happens, you won't have a ready answer. The best thing to do here is first request a time-out to consider the situation. Think creatively and involve your team if you have one. Second, if you do not come up with anything, you will need to alert the other party. You will want to engage their help in finding a way forward. They will want to do this because they too want an agreement.

This is what Fisher and Ury, the authors of *Getting to Yes*, call 'inventing options for mutual gain'. Work together to find alternative ways forward that both parties can agree to. The more options you can find, the better the end solution is likely to be.

Split the process into stages, for:

- Thinking creatively to generate ideas. At this stage, avoid judging an idea. It may be flawed, but there may be ways to improve on the details.

- Evaluating those ideas. This should be based on objective criteria that reflect the level of overlap of interests of the two parties.

- Deciding which to pursue. This must be a mutual decision, because otherwise any subsequent negotiation will be founded on shaky ground.

Resolution: finding a way through

When there is little left to work on, beyond minor details that both parties are confident about, you are into Act 3 of the bargaining step, resolution. This is largely about tying up loose ends. This can be frustrating. After a lot of major progress in Act 2, it now feels like you are moving at a snail's pace.

Things can go wrong if you try to rush. An ill-chosen statement or a moment of frustration can rub the other party up the wrong way and cause a setback that returns you to confrontation. Stay alert, confident and respectful. Take breaks when you get stuck. And trust the process. You will make progress and you will reach an agreement.

Throughout the bargaining step, ensure that you and the other party allow time to pause, take stock and summarize where you have got to. This is especially helpful if one of you has identified a sticking point that you both recognize you need to resolve.

Top tip

Keep a whiteboard, flip chart or virtual notepad visible throughout the negotiation. At each summary point, make a note of what new items you have agreed on. Maybe also record issues you need to resolve between you.

If you don't do this, make a note in your own notebook, and perhaps say out loud something like: 'I've recorded this concession [and describe it] we have just agreed on. Now I'm ready to move on.' Check that everyone around the table agrees with you and suggest that they also write exactly the same thing in their notes.

Pausing to reflect and summarize has several purposes:

1 Pausing and reflecting slows the process and allows unconscious thoughts the time to rise to conscious level.

2 Pauses also release some of the stress and dissipate adrenalin. This will relax both parties and leave them with clearer, calmer minds.

3 The summaries allow both parties to check that they have a shared understanding of where they have reached, what they have agreed so far and what is next on the agenda. Each shared understanding of the position is another step towards a final agreement.

4 The summary process prevents misunderstandings from persisting. The longer a misunderstanding lasts, the more choices will be based upon it, compounding its impact.

5 And summaries also underline the progress that you have made. Nothing is more motivating than seeing progress and acknowledging success.

Bargaining checklist

Here is a list of features of an agreement that people and organizations value. Each one represents a possible source of requests, offers or concessions:

1 Safety	8 Appearance
2 Security	9 Innovation
3 Compliance	10 Risk
4 Convenience	11 Delivery
5 Performance	12 Price
6 Durability	13 Value
7 Sustainability	14 Delight

Resolution: wrap-up

In drama, the last part of the third act is sometimes called the 'dénouement'. This is the part of a drama where everything becomes clear to the protagonists. All questions are answered and there are no surprises left in store. Narratively, it just needs one party to summarize the final state and for the other to accept that summary.

But…

The negotiation isn't over yet. It's not enough to share an understanding of where you are. Both parties must formally agree. This is where Step 3, bargain, ends. Now you need to close.

Summary points

- The bargaining step begins with each party understanding and assessing the meaning of each other's opening positions.

- Based on this assessment, you will review your fundamental negotiating strategy and decide whether you will negotiate hard, make easy concessions, walk away, compromise to get an agreement or collaborate for a win-win.

- There will be obstacles and disagreements along the way. Use the 'divide up the pie' approach to minimize the area of disagreement.

- Make and respond to requests and counteroffers. Where you don't have a response to a situation, work with the other party to find creative options that you can both gain from.

- Throughout the bargaining stage, use pauses to relax and to recognize and summarize your progress.

- The bargaining step ends with both parties sharing a common understanding of where you have reached in responding to every issue and concern.

06
Close
If it isn't right, it isn't finished

We can compare the Close step of the negotiation process to how drivers handle a junction. As you near the junction, there should be signs that tell you that it's coming up. You need to be alert for them. And you also need to signal to other road users that you are approaching the junction and preparing to stop. This is why cars have brake lights.

When you reach the junction, you need to stop and look around carefully, to check that it is safe to proceed. If it is, then you should move on.

But wait! If something goes wrong, you need to be able to execute an emergency stop. If there is an incident, you will need to deal with it accordingly. Only then can you proceed – or not. Hopefully, though, there is no problem. So, proceed with your attention focused on the road ahead.

These are the elements of the Close step in the negotiating process, and we'll look at them one at a time.

Signpost the junction

We left the negotiation process at the wrap-up. Both parties know where they are, and it feels like there is nothing left to discuss. But there's a problem that many negotiators encounter.

Because you have made good progress and built a strong working relationship, it can feel uncomfortable to try to close the deal.

Often, even experienced negotiators fear that something will go wrong and the magic will evaporate.

But, of course, if you don't close, there is no agreement. So you need to do it in a way that will not break the rapport you have with each other and damage the relationship. You need to see a 'no' as a process step rather than as a rejection.

So, before you make a close, signpost that you think that a close might be available. Start by suggesting that you think the negotiation is nearing a close and offer to summarize where you think the parties are. Cover all the important components that you believe you can both agree on.

As you do this, watch their reaction. If you find something that remains outstanding, you can revert to negotiating for a resolution. But, if not, review all the issues that either party has raised and look for confirmation that you are both satisfied with how you have resolved them.

Do the same with the concessions. Check each concession you think you have secured from your counterparty to ensure they agree that they have made the concession. Then go through the concessions you have made and check that there is nothing on the other party's list that you had not agreed to.

Finally, ask if there is anything you have left out of your summary. If there is, you'll need to go back and discuss that. If there is not, you may be ready for a trial close.

Stop and observe

You may need to simply stop talking and see how the other party responds to your summary. This is what we can call a 'silent trial close'. However, they may need a gentle nudge. The sort of questions you might ask are:

- 'Do you think we are ready to make an agreement?'
- 'Are you happy that we're in a position to agree?'
- 'Is there anything else we need to do before agreeing?'

How the other party responds to this will tell you whether it is safe to make a close.

Proceed

So, you have got there. You are as sure as you can be that your close will meet with a positive response, so it's time to summon your confidence and proceed.

How you seek formal agreement will depend on your personal style, your reading of the other person's (or team's) preferences, and any cultural norms. In general, a good way to close is to repeat the key points of the agreement you think you have reached and then make a direct close by saying something like:

- 'Can we agree on this?'
- 'I can agree to this, can you?'
- 'Will you join me in committing to this?'

The first thing to do after asking the question is to shut up and wait patiently for an answer.

Treat anything that is not a clear and unambiguous 'yes' as a 'no'. If there is any reservation in their words, their voice or their manner, it is better to understand and resolve this now than to risk buyer's remorse. This is where one party later regrets the agreement that they have made. They may not renege on that deal, but they might hold it against you, damaging the long-term relationship and the chances of future beneficial agreements.

High-integrity negotiation means ensuring both parties are equally confident that the agreement works to their benefit. If this means taking time to allow the other party to think, discuss and decide, or to reopen the conversation about a part of the agreement, this is time well spent.

Closing gambits

As a result of my advocacy for high-integrity negotiation, I am not a big fan of 'closing gambits'. These are small linguistic tactics (or maybe 'tricks') to help the other party agree when you make a close. However, what you feel comfortable using is your choice, so I offer these to you to use at your own discretion. You must, however, reconcile them with your own, and your employer's, ethical framework:

1 **Direct close**
   The simplest, and therefore often the best close is a direct close: 'We have reached our final position. Let's agree on this formally and move ahead on it.' You can slow this down and make it a little less direct by starting with a summary of where you are, before asking for the close: 'So, we have agreed… Shall we formalize this as an agreement?'

2 **Looking for the problem**
   With this type of close, you assume that there is agreement, but you offer your counterparty an opportunity to raise a concern or expose their objections. For example, you could say something like, 'Please tell me if I am wrong, but I think we have an agreement.'

3 **Creating momentum**
   Physical movement and clear intent can set up the expectation that we should comply and mirror the actions. Getting up from the table, smiling, approaching the other person and saying 'let's shake hands on this' will get you quickly to an understanding of the situation. They may say 'yes', get up and shake your hand. If they do not, either saying 'no', 'no, not yet' or 'maybe', you know there is work to do.

4 **Lightening the mood**
   Since everyone feels a little uncomfortable as you approach the close, it can help to break the mood with humour. But you must be careful to understand the culture and what humour is

likely to work. An ironic use of a cheesy closing line can spark smiles all round or, at worst, cause offence: 'I like the colour of your eyes, but I like the colour of your money even more – let's do this!'

5 **Offering equally satisfactory alternatives**
This is the negotiating equivalent to asking a small child, 'Do you want to tidy your bedroom before supper, or afterwards?' Both options work for you, but they offer the child a choice. We often reject something if we feel forced into it. So, if at the end of a negotiation, you can save two small concessions or alternative options for the close, you can offer the other party two alternatives and ask them which they want: 'Shall we agree on…, or would you prefer to agree on…?' If they choose to accept one, you have your close and can say, 'Great! We are agreed.' Of course, this can be manipulative. So use it with care.

6 **Triggering the sunk cost concern**
You and the other party have invested a lot of time, mental energy and even emotion into the negotiation. It can feel hard to abandon that and walk away. Gently reminding your counterparty of all the effort they have committed can trigger fears of losing all that work, or needing to commit to a whole lot more. And that can help them feel that the time is right to close.

7 **The scarcity effect**
Scarcity is one of the most common ways marketers and salespeople trigger a buying decision. Whether it's scarcity of product ('only three remaining') or time ('sale ends on Sunday'), it's very familiar. It can feel uncomfortable but it certainly works. Put simply, people have a fear of missing out (FOMO). If you threaten to walk away from further negotiations, the other party may fear losing all the concessions they have and see the value of the deal they have negotiated.

8 **The one last push**
You might sense that you are nearly there, but not quite. You sense that there's one more thing the other party might need

to feel comfortable with agreeing. In this case, you might close with something like this: 'If I were to offer this, would you be able to agree to everything else we've discussed?' Or maybe a question like, 'What is it you need to complete an agreement?' Asking a question never hurts. Another way to do it is to take responsibility for agreeing: 'We need to make an agreement. I can agree if...' This is sometimes known as the conditional close. This is where you suggest one more condition and invite your counterparty to accept that final condition.

One last thing to add. If you look at sales books and courses, you can find dozens of closes, with each one a little more manipulative than the last. Many are simply variants on these. For most workplace negotiations, however, you don't need to use clever closes and they will often be counterproductive.

Once you have a confirmation that both parties agree, the extent and manner of formalizing it will depend entirely on the context and culture. It may be anything from a simple handshake to the completion of a contract. Because you have done your preparation (step 1 of the negotiating process), you will know what is appropriate and be ready to execute it.

Emergency stop

But wait! What happens if the other party says no and is not ready to close? Stop. Do not try to hassle them and certainly avoid getting frustrated. It's just part of the process. They may be playing games, but the safest assumption to work with is that you have missed something.

Clearly there is a gap in the framework you have negotiated. So, the best mindset to have is curiosity. Ask open questions about where the other party is, and what they need to resolve, before they will feel ready to close an agreement. Then listen patiently, giving them time to explain their position.

This is a tricky time. As with dangerous road situations, after you have stopped and evaluated the situation, proceed with great caution.

In Chapter 14, Problems, we will look at getting stuck, when there is a small problem to resolve, and deadlock, where objections seem to have caused an intractable issue. But, to keep the road junction metaphor going, let's get ready to move on.

Eyes on the road ahead

What should you do and say, once you have agreement? This is a trick question because the ideal answer is '**nothing**'.

You have what you want. Anything you do or say now won't be needed to get agreement and cannot get you a better one. So, the best case will be 'no change'. More likely, because saying and doing things usually has consequences, those consequences will be bad. You may sow the seeds of doubt, cause a worry that a better deal was available, give offence, or even trigger a withdrawal from the agreement.

This has a name: 'buying back the deal'.

Scary examples of buying back the deal

If you have a strong constitution, here are some horror stories of negotiations turning 180 degrees because a negotiator thought that one last comment would help:

- 'You'll be so glad you agreed to this, it will make you the first organization to partner with us on this.'
  - o 'What? You didn't tell us you have never tried this!'

- 'Thank you. My boss will be delighted we have this agreement.'
  - o 'Really? It sounds like we may have conceded too much to you.'
- 'Great! I just need you to also agree...'
  - o 'No way. I'm out!'

Don't buy back the deal. Once you have agreed, there are only two things you should say and do. These are concerned solely with:

1 The administration and details of the agreement you have made: next steps, contract signing, logistic arrangements and other practicalities. These are things that start from the agreement and move the relationship and arrangements forward.

2 The courtesies of leaving the negotiation politely, according to good manners in the relevant culture.

Summary points

- People often fear the closing stage of a negotiation. They worry it will break the magic spell of rapport.
- Signpost that you think agreement is near by summarizing your understanding of the situation and looking for confirmation.
- Observe the response you get. If necessary, make a trial close.
- The best close for a negotiation is a direct close, simply asking the other party if they are ready to confirm their agreement.
- If the answer is no (or a qualified yes), ask questions to discover what you need to fix to get an agreement.
- Once you have an agreement, avoid buying back the deal by saying or doing anything that could possibly create doubt.

07

Follow-up

For the want of a nail, a kingdom was lost

You have done a good thing. You have created an agreement with someone else that will give benefits to both sides of the agreement. You might argue that follow-up should not be a step in the negotiation, but a process for after the negotiation. That's fine. But it is essential for the long-term success of the negotiation. So, now what you need to do is capitalize on your success.

Details matter

It's amazing how much the small things matter. That's probably why we have so many sayings and expressions that sum it up, like 'cutting corners' or 'cheap is dear'. So, it shouldn't be necessary to list the reasons why follow-up is important. However, here are some of the main ones.

First and foremost is the need to avoid throwing away all the value you generated by defaulting on your obligations or upsetting the other party. On the flip side is the fact that if you do not follow up properly, it creates the impression that you don't care, which the other side may interpret as permission to not honour their commitments.

However, this is the bare minimum. That is not a standard a professional person should hold themselves to. When you go beyond a minimum compliance and follow up diligently and efficiently, it will build trust and strengthen the relationship.

The true value of a negotiated agreement exceeds the agreement itself; it can be a gateway to more and better agreements. This is why the strategy of making easy concessions can work. It is the concept of a loss leader in sales, in which a product or service is sold at a loss to engage a new customer with the hope of winning repeat business and a profitable long-term relationship.

Making the agreement work

Mindset is key to the successful follow-up of a negotiated agreement. This is not mere admin, nor a nuisance to be complied with. Instead, see this as the real work of delivering on your promise and building a professional or commercial relationship.

This means you need to adopt a long-term focus. You want to make your agreement sustainable so that it holds firm until each party has delivered every commitment. And through doing this, you want to craft a durable relationship that can survive and thrive despite (and perhaps because of) the inevitable disagreements and conflicting priorities along the way. Your end goal must be a platform for further agreements that will benefit both parties.

In addition to this long-term strategic orientation, there are other aspects of your mindset that will serve you well in serving the agreement well. Let's look at six that can make a particular contribution.

Communication

First is a commitment to communicating often and well with the other party. Good communication is essential for trust, and not just for the obvious reason of transparency. One component of trust is the extent to which someone believes that you are reliable in doing what you have promised to do. But it is not enough to only *be* reliable. If you commit to do something that will take you three weeks, some people will wonder, part way through the second week, whether you are really doing it. If you are, how do they know? Be proactive in your communicating your progress.

Proactivity

This brings us nicely on to proactivity as a general mindset. There will be problems along the way of making an agreement work. The longer you leave a problem, the more likely it is to get worse. So, instead, take control. Have the courage to do what you need to do, and let the other party know there is a problem and that you're dealing with it. If they hear about the problem from someone else, that can undermine trust.

Collaboration

A collaborative mindset sees the counterparty to your agreement as a partner in resolving these problems. Work together, listening to their point of view and accessing their experience and wisdom.

Flexibility

As you tackle the day-to-day issues and the big, scary problems, be as flexible as possible. Distinguish between the goals and commitments that are a part of the agreement and the ways and means of achieving them. Being prepared to change approach and adapt to circumstance is a key aspect of a solution-focused mindset.

Generosity

A lot of sales and customer care training talks about a 'customer-centric' mindset. But for negotiations, thinking of the partner to your agreement in this way creates a mental separation that can be unhelpful. So, instead, adopt a generosity mindset. Where issues arise, be ready to make generous gestures if they can help resolve the situation. What you'll find is that most human beings will reciprocate this kind of generosity when the opportunity arises. The extent to which they do this will help you frame any future negotiations.

Continuous improvement

Finally, a continuous improvement mindset will help you steer away from the zone of complacency where serving your agreement feels easy or automatic. This can be a major hazard. Complacency creates confirmation bias. That is, we think everything is fine so, when we look, that is what we see. We fail to notice the first signs of problems – like a partner who is not as happy as we think they 'should' be. Continuously ask yourself and your team, 'How can we do this better, to become more efficient, more effective and give greater delight to our partner?'

Your to-do list

Your follow-up tasks fall neatly into five sections:

1 Immediate tasks: completing the agreement admin
2 You and your team
3 Actions under the agreement
4 Managing the relationship
5 End of the agreement

The following sections look at what you need to consider under each of these themes. There is also a handy checklist in Appendix 4.

Immediate tasks: completing the agreement admin

Let's get started by reducing the scope for misunderstandings and disputes. If your agreement is not subject to contract, it still pays to document it in writing, even if all you use is a simple exchange of emails.

Share the written reflection of your agreement with the other party, not as a consultation, but as a record of what you agreed. But ask them to read it to confirm that this is their understanding too. If it is not, agree amendments and re-circulate it.

This is your best hope to ensure alignment, and the more contract-like it is, the more solid the framework will be. Aim to secure a written confirmation that they accept the document as a true representation of what they have agreed. When you have it, date it and file it securely.

You and your team

If you have worked with a team to secure an agreement that benefits your organization, function or department, it's time to thank them for their work and support. Thank the team as a whole and thank individuals.

Conduct a team retrospective review of performance with a focus on the lessons you can each learn to develop your professional practice in the future. Use a similar format to the team review that you'll find in Chapter 12, Teamworking.

If individual team members have committed a substantial amount of time or effort to the negotiation, it is good practice to meet them individually to offer recognition for their work, praise for their contributions and offer developmental feedback to help them grow professionally. If you do not have a line management responsibility for them, it is still good to do this, but you can also send a summary of your performance assessment to their immediate manager.

In all of this, do not forget yourself! Indeed, many negotiations will be one-to-one conversations with no team involved. So, after reaching agreement, take some time to reflect on your performance. Think about how you:

- prepared
- conducted yourself
- assessed the other party
- responded to circumstances
- made decisions along the way
- participated in the close

Also consider the outcome and the extent to which, in retrospect, it was the best you could have achieved. Why not make a note in your journal about what you learned and how you would handle a similar negotiation next time.

Actions under the agreement

At the heart of your follow-up is the long list of actions that the agreement requires of you. You will also want to track the performance of the other party in attending to their commitments. Create your own follow-up checklist and schedule, starting with the formal requirements and any milestone dates. Add enabling tasks and checkpoints along the way. There is no right or wrong format, so devise an approach that you think will work for you and then evolve and improve it as you go. You may find some software or a simple calendar or to-do app will suit you.

If you are working with a team, you will want to add role allocations and responsibilities to the plan. A good tip is to prepare a master schedule or checklist and then extract from it a personalized version for each member of the team. Once again, there are plenty of collaboration tools that make this very easy. All this will help you keep your agreement on track and spot issues early on.

It's no good having a plan unless you also carry out the actions that you have agreed to and documented in the plan. And here's your reminder to remind your colleagues of any actions that they need to carry out too. As things get done, make sure there is a record of their completion and that all parties that need to be, are aware of it. Sometimes a record of compliance can become valuable, should there be a dispute.

Finally for this section, monitor the performance, both of your team if you have one, and of the counterparty and their team if they have one. Close monitoring allows you to identify and work on problems early on, before they become bigger and more complex than they need to be. A no-blame culture is best. When something goes wrong, focus on finding the cause, fixing the problem and amending or creating processes to prevent recurrence.

Managing the relationship

At the core of any agreement is the relationship between the parties to the agreement. As soon as you have closed, thank the person or people with whom you have negotiated. This is a common courtesy which emphasizes a positive approach to the long-term relationship. Send them a polite note and if it is printed (or, better, handwritten) rather than emailed, it will have more impact.

Use that note to tell them you enjoyed the process and thank them for handling it well. And, of course, also say that you are looking forward to working with them to bring the agreement to life and to build on your relationship.

It might be appropriate to offer feedback, depending on the circumstances. What was the negotiation about and what is the formal nature of your relationship? If it was about forming a working agreement with a colleague, for example, then feedback can be appropriate and might be welcome, if you offer it. But never impose feedback on someone unless you have a supervisory relationship. If you do it well, good feedback can enhance trust and help the other person to develop their professional skills.

As you work on delivering the terms of the agreement, take every opportunity to nurture your relationships. Communicate often and look for the chance to speak in person, rather than hiding behind email. This can be difficult in a modern hybrid work-place where people are based in different places or work outside of the office. Even video calls are better than email.

Regular check-ins to discuss what's happening are the best way to head off misunderstandings, confusion and disputes. But disagreements may occur and these can lead to conflict. So, tackle them as soon as you spot the warning signs. If you have a written record of the agreement, this can be a valuable asset in dispute resolution. But beware: rushing to quote written terms will not endear you to anyone. Use this as a fall-back option only.

End of agreement

Your agreement will come to an end, either because it is time-con-strained or because you have each discharged all your commit-ments. This is a point to meet up and confirm to one another that this is the case and discuss the extent to which the agreement has delivered what each of you had intended when you entered into it.

It's also the time for one last 'end-of-agreement' review – either with your team or by self-reflection. What did you learn from the whole process?

Finally, if you have not been doing so already, set up a meeting with your partner to discuss the future of your relationship, and any potential new agreements you could form that could benefit you both and bring your relationship even closer.

Summary points

- Proper follow-up will optimize the outcomes you can achieve from your negotiated agreement.

- A good mindset for following up includes a long-term strategic orientation, a commitment to frequent and effective communication, a proactive and collaborative mindset, a sense of flexibility and of generosity, and a determination to improve continuously.

- The immediate follow-up tasks are documenting and seeking approval for the record of the agreement.

- You need to thank your team if you had one and ensure that you and your team can reflect on and learn from the negotiation process.

- Plan, track and monitor the actions you committed to under the agreement.

- Thank the other party for their conduct of the negotiation and use this to grow and develop your relationship.

- Formally note the end of the agreement and conduct a final end-of-agreement review.

Part 2
Negotiation skills

08
Analysis
There's nothing more useful than a good model

In Chapter 3, we saw the need for effective preparation for your negotiation. A large part of this step is about understanding the situation. To support you in doing this, there is a wide range of tools and models. An important part of my own philosophy of training, writing and educating is what I call my 'toolbox approach'. As an educator, the more tools I can give you for your toolbox, the more likely you will be to have just the right tool for each situation you encounter.

Some of the tools you learn about in this book and elsewhere will be interesting to you, but may never turn out to find a use in the work you are doing. But just knowing that they are there can give you reassurance that, if you meet a new situation, you are likely to be able to handle it.

So, here are the tools I think managers and other professionals will find most useful in preparing for a negotiation.

Negotiation toolbox

Mind map

A mind map is one of the most widely useful tools. It is great for many things, like:

- organizing ideas and information
- understanding and sharing information
- assisting memory or recall

It is the first of these that makes it particularly helpful for analysing a negotiation before starting it. Start with a large sheet of blank paper and place your central concept in the middle. I like to use the goal of my negotiation to focus my mind.

From this, you can build a web of ideas surrounding the central concept. And ideas that relate to these surround them. Use lines to connect related ideas and very soon you will see why these are also called spider diagrams or concept maps.

There are no rules, but using colours, shapes, pictures and icons will make the map more compelling and the ideas easy to remember. It allows you to get all your different ideas on one sheet of paper and arrange them so that lines and proximity represent how they relate to one another.

There are software tools for creating these, but there's a benefit in drawing and re-drawing these maps on paper. Working this way makes the thought process more intimate and drawing by hand helps embody your understanding.

SWOT analysis

A well-known tool for assessing your situation in a wide range of contexts is a SWOT analysis. In the context of negotiation, you will identify your:

Strengths going into the negotiation. This is your leverage over the other party.

Weaknesses going into the negotiation. This is the leverage they have over you.

Opportunities that the negotiation offers.

Threats – things that could go wrong for you.

Figure 8.1 Mind map of negotiation

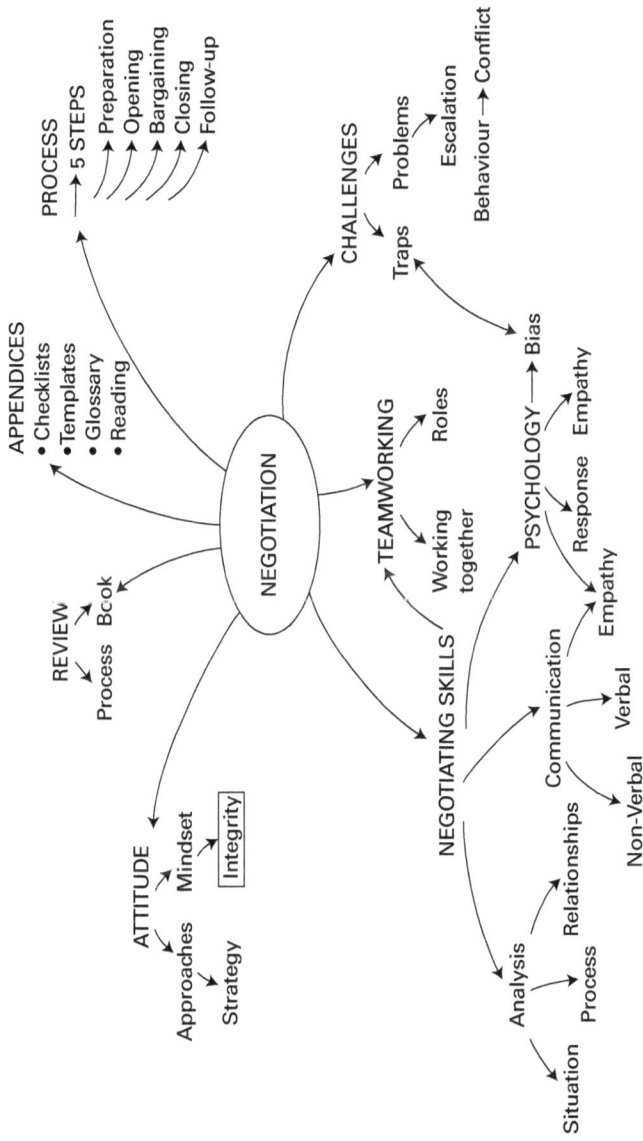

When you have done this, you can use it to derive tactics or strategies to:

- deploy your strengths to harness your opportunities and counter the threats;
- reduce or work around your weaknesses.

SPECTRES analysis

There are many frameworks to help with spotting opportunities, threats and trends. These are a helpful supplement to SWOT analysis. The best known are PEST analysis and its extension, PESTLE analysis. My own variant is SPECTRES analysis: it helps you see the spectres of the future. You'll be able to figure what the acronyms PEST and PESTLE could stand for from the following description of SPECTRES (or you can look in the Glossary in Appendix 7).

When looking for threats or opportunities on the horizon, we consider trends relating to:

- Society, social and cultural pressures, and relationships.
- Political factors like positions, agendas and webs of influence. Remember that politics exists wherever different people are working on the same thing.
- Economic and financial matters, both at the macro scale and at the scale of your business, project or even team.
- Commercial and competitive pressures, for each party to the negotiation.
- Technology and technical advancements are a rich source of opportunities and threats.
- Regulation, legislation and policy constraints change constantly and can drive behaviours which, if you aren't aware of these underlying causes, can seem odd.
- Ethical, environmental and sustainability concerns need to be paramount in our minds.

- Safety, security and wellbeing imperatives should always drive decision-making.

Pros and cons analysis

There are lots of variants on the simple approach of making a list of positive and negative, or good and bad, consequences of a particular choice or decision. At its simplest, this is a two-column table.

But we can add an extra column to recognize that there are some consequences that are important, but neither good nor bad. These observations can sometimes lead to a new insight and a creative solution. I recommend you always include this column, between the other two, to avoid the trap of getting caught in binary ('yes or no', 'this or that') thinking. This idea comes from Edward de Bono's 1982 book, *De Bono's Thinking Course*, and it appears several times in his writing as the PMI Technique, standing for Plus, Minus and Interesting.

We can further extend the idea by adding tactical columns to document ideas for how to mitigate disadvantages and optimize advantages.

You can also think of pros and cons in terms of forces that would drive you to do something or restrain you from doing another thing. For example:

- forces that would drive you to accept an offer, and the forces that restrain you from accepting it;
- forces that would drive you to make a concession, and the forces that drive you to reject a request for it.

The Pareto Principle

The Italian economist Vilfredo Pareto gave his name to the Pareto Principle, which is perhaps better known as the 80:20 rule. Whilst the numbers 80 and 20 are not always appropriate, there are a wide range of contexts in which a large majority of impacts arise from a small number of factors.

Pareto's original observation was that around 80 per cent of the wealth of early 20th-century Italy was in the hands of around 20 per cent of the population. This relationship still holds for global wealth and arises because of the power law nature of wealth in human societies.

It also seems to be common that a large part of the benefit of a negotiation can come from a small number of highly salient factors. So it is a useful analytical technique to:

- list all the concessions you could seek to win
- put a value on each
- list them in value order
- identify the top few that contribute around 80 per cent of the total potential value (likely around one-fifth – 20 per cent – of them)
- focus your negotiating strategy on winning these concessions

When you have done this, repeat the exercise for the concessions the other party might ask of you. They will be focusing on the high-value ones and you will want to work hard to defend those that are also high cost to you.

MoSCoW / KYIV analysis

The Pareto Principle is at the heart of the widely known and used MoSCoW analysis. This is another way to prioritize among the long list of things you may want to achieve in your negotiation. It rates importance on a four-point scale that gives us the MSCW acronym that lends the method its name.

Musts are the things that you must have. The driving purpose of the negotiation is to achieve them. If you cannot secure all your 'musts', the negotiation will not have been worthwhile. Your musts are therefore closely related to your BATNA. If the negotiation doesn't deliver your 'musts', then you will need to revert to your best alternative to a negotiated agreement that does deliver them.

Shoulds are the second category of objectives to achieve. These are the things that a successful negotiation will also deliver and so are linked to a good, but not optimum, outcome. Your 'shoulds' are not critical to you, but you will aim to secure them because of the high level of value they can deliver.

Coulds are the things that, if you can get them, will make the outcome even better. Securing all your 'coulds' is pretty much a best-case scenario. You will be able to consider the negotiation a success if you get all of your 'musts' and most of your 'shoulds', but fail to secure any of the 'coulds'. But it is worth putting in some extra effort to try to deliver some or all your 'coulds'.

Won'ts are different. You can think of these as the things that you would get if you could get them, but you know that the effort to get them, and the concessions you'll need to make, are not justified by the value of these things. So, you should not waste your time and your negotiating collateral in pursuit of these. Take them off your list of objectives. If one drops into your lap, that's a bonus!

You can think of a Moscow analysis as deriving from the Pareto principle. This is the idea that you get 80 per cent of the benefit from 20 per cent of the concessions. Your 'musts' are the vital few things that will deliver a big part of the benefit, and your 'shoulds' may be at the 80:20 point. The numbers in the figure are purely illustrative, but it shows clearly how it would take a whole lot of work to win a marginal extra benefit from the 'won'ts'.

For people who want an alternative version, there is also KYIV analysis, in which there are also four categories:

Keep for sure

Yes, if we possibly can

If we get the chance, we will

Very unlikely – don't pursue

Figure 8.2   MoSCoW analysis and the Pareto Principle

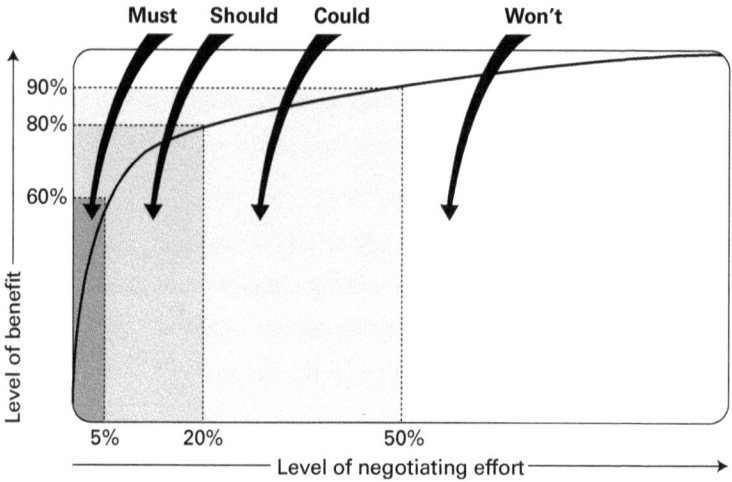

Prioritization map

An alternative way to prioritize negotiating objectives – or anything else – is a prioritization map that charts benefits or value against a measure of cost, difficulty or risk.

High-value, low-effort negotiation objectives are top priority. But always check that you are not missing something important, because if these options seem too good to be true, there is a chance they are. But, where you can find a risk-reward imbalance in your favour, you should pursue the opportunity with vigour.

Low-value, high-effort objectives are simply not worth pursuing. You could spend a lot of time and incur major risks, and have little or nothing to show for your work. This would be wasted effort.

Low-value, low-effort objectives are the quick wins. They are worth pursuing because the risk and return are in proportion. But the ease of tackling these can be seductive, and each win is a small one. This means you can dissipate a lot of energy chasing not a lot.

Figure 8.3   Prioritization map

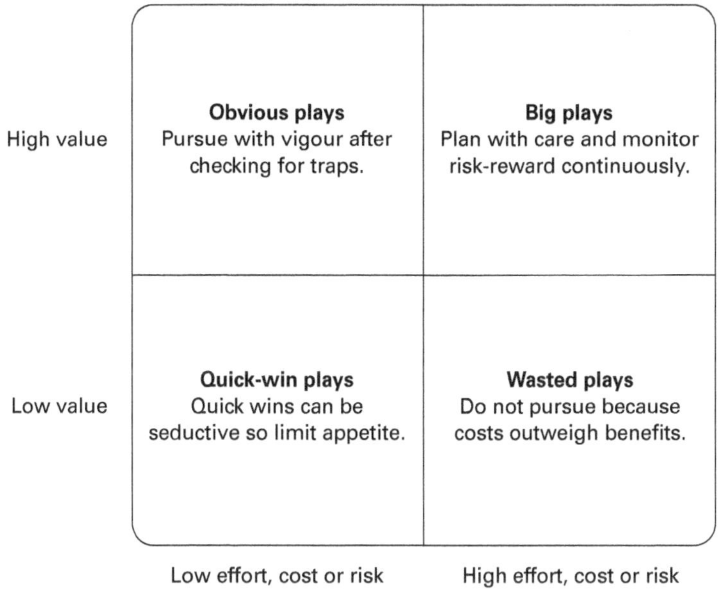

	Low effort, cost or risk	High effort, cost or risk
High value	**Obvious plays** Pursue with vigour after checking for traps.	**Big plays** Plan with care and monitor risk-reward continuously.
Low value	**Quick-win plays** Quick wins can be seductive so limit appetite.	**Wasted plays** Do not pursue because costs outweigh benefits.

But, as a way of making progress in your negotiation, these can be invaluable.

The trickiest objectives to evaluate are those that offer a big opportunity but will require a corresponding amount of effort. You cannot afford the resources to pursue many of these, so choose your objectives with care and plan your strategy scrupulously. Maintain a watchful eye for shifts in the balance and be prepared to step away if the risk-reward balance shifts against you.

Leverage matrix

Like the prioritization map above, a leverage matrix is a two-by-two map. This gives negotiating strategies for different terms or concessions based on how much leverage the negotiator has.

Figure 8.4   Leverage matrix

	Low leverage	High leverage
High importance factor	**Collaborate** Work with the counterparty to try to secure the concessions that you need, using anything you can.	**Hold** Stay committed to winning the concessions that you need, using your strong leverage.
Low importance factor	**Concede** Walk away from these terms and let your counterparty have a win, because you cannot.	**Trade** Exchange concessions here to increase leverage on more important terms (top left).

Stay committed to winning concessions on high-importance negotiating objectives where you have a lot of leverage. Obviously, do not get caught up in overcommitting your negotiating capital, but these are concessions you should win.

On the other hand, there is little point pursuing low-value objectives where you don't have much leverage. Put up a small show of resistance but be prepared to let your counterparty win these and feel good.

There may be some low-importance terms that you could win easily. But you may want to trade these wins to support you in winning other, more important concessions.

These high-importance terms are ones where you may not have enough leverage to win them easily. Deploy every resource you have and be prepared to work hard and collaboratively to find a way to secure what you need.

Discounted cash flow (DCF)

A discounted cash flow (DCF) is the most thorough way to evaluate the financial impact, over a long period of time, of a series of costs and benefits. It takes full account of the impacts of projected inflation and interest rates, to calculate a measure of the return on one or more investments.

The measures you will most often work with are net present value (NPV) and internal rate of return (IRR). Both give you the same information in a different form. The mathematics and spreadsheet modelling of a DCF is beyond the scope of this book to describe and you might want to seek out a financial analyst to work with. But, in summary:

1 You need assumptions for the long-term deposit interest rate your organization could secure and the rate of inflation over the period of the model. Organizations often have standard rates they apply to their models.

2 You then convert each benefit and cost into a financial figure and profile these over time: yearly, quarterly or monthly.

3 By applying a discount rate (based on the inflation and interest rate assumptions), you can render each receipt or expense into a value in present-day terms (a present value, or PV).

4 Adding all the PVs up (negative for costs and positive for income), you get an NPV that is a good measure of the value of the agreement you have modelled.

5 You can also calculate an IRR which is the equivalent to the rate you would need to get if you made the investments into a simple interest-bearing account and drew down the income in the model.

REAL-WORLD EXAMPLE
Using a DCF to inform a negotiation

At the start of my career, I worked with a team that advised on negotiations for the purchase of large amounts of housing stock from English local authorities by housing associations. Each party to the negotiation needed to form an opinion of the value of the housing stock under a range of scenarios, to inform their negotiations over headline price and specific terms. They would each commission a 30-year DCF model, into which they could then input a range of scenarios. Producing those models involved researching a wide range of assumptions and setting up different combinations to represent each scenario.

Value and ROI calculations

Calculating the value of different options for your negotiation will also be important. In the BATNA section of Chapter 3, Prepare, we saw different ways to calculate value, and the importance of the measure called return on investment (ROI). There is no need to repeat that here.

Scenario planning

Scenario planning is an analytical process of identifying a range of potential scenarios and planning what you would do if they came to pass. Typically, you would work with three to five scenarios that would include a:

- **Best case** – meeting, and maybe exceeding, your negotiating goal.
- **Worst case** – this should be your best alternative to a negotiated agreement (BATNA), because you can always walk away and

accept this. But you may want to consider your options if you find the negotiation hovering around your BATNA.

- **Likely case** or maybe a best reasonable case.

And maybe a couple of unusual but plausible scenarios, such as a disaster scenario, where your BATNA ceases to be available and you need to consider your WATNA, or worst alternative to a negotiated agreement.

We don't do scenario planning because we expect to accurately anticipate what will happen as one of our scenarios. Rather, it is a way of thinking through some of the developments that might arise during your negotiation process, and the flexibility and resources we have to respond.

Decision tree

Decision trees are one step on from a scenario analysis and look at options for 'if this happens, what will we do then?' They are hard to prepare and can rapidly become out of date if the negotiating situation evolves in a direction that you had not anticipated. But the principle is simple.

You anticipate a number of possible decisions you might face. For each one, you consider what different situations might prevail and, for each situation, you determine what decisions you could take for best advantage. Where you can, identify how one decision might link to the next.

The reason you may want to do this, in a limited way at least, is because it allows you and your team to consider situations, and the choices you'll face, without time pressure or the impact of negotiating room emotions. And, even if the real decisions turn out to be different to those you planned for, there is a good chance that some of the considerations will overlap. You will probably have discussed and gamed out some of the issues you need to resolve.

Concession schedules

Another tool for dealing with multiple scenarios is to create two schedules for concessions that could arise in the bargaining step of the negotiation. These would cover:

1 the concessions you might be asked to make and the costs and implications for each;

2 the concessions you might ask for and the benefits each would offer you.

This is a way to document the value of each move you might choose to make during the negotiation. You can combine this by categorizing each using the MoSCoW framework:

1 concessions requests that you must, should, could and probably won't reject;

2 concessions you must, should, could and won't seek from the other party.

It can also be helpful to look at each of these schedules from the perspective of your counterparty. How would they value each concession? You can make a lot of progress if you can identify a concession that is easy for you to make but has a lot of value to the other side, or a request that they can meet with little cost, that gives you a big benefit.

Influence map

Your counterparty may be negotiating under the influence of a wide variety of possibly competing pressures, coming from multiple directions, like:

- inside their organization – possibly from different constituencies, like operations, support, finance or HR

- customers and clients – who may represent different pressures

- business partners, suppliers and distributors

- regulators or accreditation, audit or assurance organizations
- competitors
- local communities and pressure groups
- staff representative bodies and trade unions

Draw up a map of all the influences you are aware of, along with any you believe could also be present. Characterize each with your assessment of:

- what pressures they create on the negotiation
- how important the negotiator will consider them to be
- the extent to which they help or hinder your own interests

Relationship mapping

Who are the players on the other side of your negotiation and how do they relate to one another? Who respects whom, who are the experts and who can impose their influence on others?

As you find out who will be present (or make assumptions about who might attend), build a picture of how these individuals might interact. A sociogram is a good tool for this – also called a social network or a relationship map.

This represents each individual as a circle on a large canvas. Use lines to connect those who know each other well, perhaps using thicker lines to represent stronger relationships and arrows to indicate the direction of influence. A bar across a line could represent a poor relationship that may have broken down.

Then you can add more individuals:

- other individuals in the negotiating team's organization who may influence the negotiation
- your own negotiating team members
- third parties, from outside the negotiation

The purpose of this chart is to help you understand the interpersonal dynamics in the room.

Figure 8.5   Illustrative sociogram

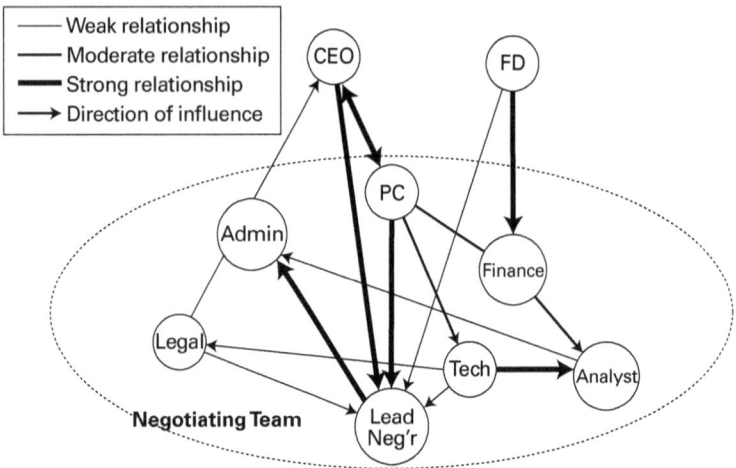

Negotiator analysis

The final analytical tool is to create an analysis of each member of the other negotiating team. Build a picture of who they are, how they think and what their point of view might be. Document anything you know about:

- their formal power and informal influence over negotiating colleagues
- their attitudes to the negotiation and the matters under discussion
- what they care about, their interests
- any history they have with the topic, with team colleagues or with members of your team
- any roles they have had or actions they have taken in the past that have a bearing on the negotiation

As the negotiation progresses, you can update this analysis and refine your understanding of individuals' responses and better plan for how to influence them.

Summary points

This summary is in the form of a checklist of analysis tools to support negotiation preparation. They are not tools that you must or even should use. Instead, they are tools to consider using.

- Mind map
- SWOT analysis
- SPECTRES analysis
- Pros and cons analysis
- The Pareto Principle
- MoSCoW/KYIV analysis
- Prioritization map
- Leverage matrix
- Discounted cash flow (DCF)
- Value and ROI calculations
- Scenario planning
- Decision tree
- Concession schedules
- Influence map
- Relationship mapping
- Negotiator analysis

09
Communication
You cannot not communicate

Whatever you do or say in a negotiation – whether with one person or a whole team across the table – the other party will interpret it as meaning something. The same is true for the things you don't do or don't say.

This means that, to master negotiation, we must also master various skills of communication:

- Choosing your non-verbal communication
- Reading non-verbal communication
- How you speak
- Use of language in spoken communication
- Questioning
- Listening
- Empathy

Choosing your non-verbal communication

You only get one chance to make a first impression.

I learned this truism from my father, and it's an important reminder that humans judge one another on first sight. So, knowing this, in formal contexts we have a chance to choose the impression we give, with our appearance and body language.

Appearance is the easier, because each instance is a one-and-done. We carry out our grooming regime and select our clothing and accessories, and we are done for the day, with little more than a quick refresh and tidy-up from time to time. Body language takes constant attention until it becomes habit.

Clothes and accessories

In choosing your clothing and accessories, there are two rules to keep in mind:

1 people like people who are like themselves, and

2 people respect people who are like they want to be

This tells us two things about what makes for appropriate choices when determining what clothes and accessories to wear for a negotiation. The first rule suggests you need to fit in by making a culturally appropriate choice. You need to fit in. Standing out is fine if you stand out as 'part of the group'. So, choose clothes that fit the context and maybe use colour and accessories that will make you a little more memorable and individual.

But be careful. If your jewellery, scarf or tie attracts more attention than you do, this may not be appropriate. Humorous ties are not for serious people and showy jewellery suggests you are more interested in your appearance than your professional role.

The second rule tells us that, to impress, it is worth stepping up a notch in the standard of your clothes and accessories. Once again, don't overdo it. But you can set yourself apart in a positive way by being just a little more smart, stylish and well-presented than the people around you.

This means thinking about the quality of your clothes and accessories, how you care for them and the way you combine them. Polish jewellery, belts and shoes. Put the right creases into suits, shirts and blouses. Tie your tie properly and arrange your scarf elegantly.

Accessories don't stop with clothing and jewellery. Think about the bag, notebook, pen, phone, tablet or laptop you use. Again, make selections of personal items that convey competence and seriousness. And look after all these items to keep them clean and tidy.

One last thing about your accessories is the choice you make about which to keep out during the negotiation, and which to either not bring, or put away. A notebook and pen communicate seriousness, attention to detail and, when you write something down, respect for what the other person says. Having a phone on the table, however, says you may be more interested in the messages or calls that might come in than you are in the negotiation.

Body language

The second aspect of appearance is your body language. This covers:

- your posture
- the way you move – or don't move
- facial expressions
- eye contact – or avoidance
- gestures

Body language is a huge topic, so let's focus on the most important aspects for effective negotiation. You want to convey interest and attention, confidence, warmth and openness.

To convey interest and attention, look at the person who is speaking, or that you are speaking to. Make good eye contact and turn your whole body towards them. If you must turn your head to look them in the eye, don't: move your whole body instead. People subconsciously notice where your feet are pointing when you are standing, or which way your body is oriented when you are seated. They interpret this as where you are unconsciously focusing your attention. The other thing they notice is fidgeting. This may not be a sign of a lack of attention, but because some people will interpret it that way, it is best to limit these kinds of movements.

Fidgeting can also come across as a sign that you lack confidence, so this is another reason to fight the fidget! Convey confidence with an upright posture, whether seated or standing. A great way to achieve this is to imagine there is a puppet string attached to the top of your head. Allow a gentle tension to lift your head lightly on your shoulders and pull your body into an upright position. Good eye contact also conveys confidence but, as with so many things, overdoing it can be a mistake. In this case it can seem creepy. The last important sign of confidence is a pleasant smile.

That smile also conveys warmth. This is where moving can help you. If you freeze all motion to control your fidgeting, you will seem cold and somewhat alien. It's not natural. Make your facial expressions animated to acknowledge and encourage the other person to speak. Use nods and gentle hand gestures to further encourage and show interest. And again, your eye contact is a route to an appropriate level of intimacy.

Finally, lean in gently towards the person you are speaking with. If you lean back too much, it can look as though you want to disengage from the conversation. This might just be your way of relaxing and thinking things through, so if you do lean back, increase your eye contact and positive signals like nods, aha sounds, smiling and eye contact. It's also dangerous to lean forward too much during a negotiation. This can come across as aggressive.

Confidence and warmth are two elements that will help you come across as trustworthy. The third is openness. The first and most important signal here is your posture. Keep your gross posture as symmetric as possible because asymmetric posture seems to incur distrust. And open your body up. Not only does a hunched and closed posture convey nervousness and doubt, but it can also signal that you have something to hide. And, although there is no scientific evidence for this, it's a common belief that people who don't make eye contact cannot be trusted. Don't let that catch you out, even if you are 100 per cent trustworthy!

Reading non-verbal communication

As big as the topic of controlling your body language is the topic of reading body language in others. However, your ability to notice and interpret nonverbal cues can give you a lot of valuable information. After all, a lot of communication is non-verbal and, as a negotiator, you need to become adept at reading it.

There is a lot of cod psychology and folk wisdom about this topic that does not stand up to the scrutiny of good evidence. But one thing you can rely on is the importance of changes. If you can observe how someone behaves in a neutral context, when they are not under pressure and can feel at ease, this will give you a valuable baseline.

After that, if you notice a change in posture, gesture, tone of voice, eye contact or any of the many body language signals, you know one thing: something has impacted that person at an emotional level. With an understanding of the context, some basic body language knowledge and a bit of detective work, you may be able to figure out something of what they are thinking.

What, you may wonder, is the basic body language knowledge you most need to know?

The most important thing to remember is that you should never jump to conclusions and think you know what's going on in someone's mind, based on one observation. Context is important, and a change may mean one of several things. A small shake of the head may signal disagreement, discomfort or confusion. Folding of arms may indicate a barrier, self-soothing, feeling cold or it may just be a comfortable way to sit. So, gather information from a whole cluster of observations. If they all lead to one conclusion, then that may be the right one.

And, even if you know what a gesture means, you still don't know why they did it. For example, leaning back often means disengaging from what is going on. But is this because the person is uninterested, offended, distracted, disagrees with you or needs to disengage to think? If they continue looking at you, they are probably still interested. If they look away, maybe they need to avoid the distraction while they consider what they have heard. This is all very tricky.

The final general tip is to try to spot muscle tone. This can be tight and clenched (where the physical tension betrays emotional tension) or relaxed. You might spot this in, for example, the gross posture, choppy or fluid gestures, tight or loose shoulders, clenched or relaxed jawline or brow.

Often, it's the smallest gestures, which we cannot easily control, that are most indicative of something. A quick raise of the eyebrow can mean curiosity – or outright disbelief. A furrow of the brow or slight closing of the eyes can mean confusion, doubt, disbelief or displeasure. If you want to know what a fleeting expression means, try making it yourself, and see how it feels. This is far more reliable than rote learning a set of 'rules'.

Another important indicator, particularly of mood, can be breathing. If you can detect someone's breathing pattern, look for two things: the depth and the pace of breathing. In general, slow breathing reflects calm; deliberate deep breaths suggest a feeling that they need to calm themselves. Shallow breathing suggests stress and rapid breathing, excitement.

Hands are also a good indicator of what is going on in somebody's mind. A clenched fist can obviously mean anger. But in other situations, it is more likely to betray frustration or signal determination. An open palm suggests a lighter mood, but look at its orientation. Open palms facing forward or upward suggest openness, honesty and a desire to placate and engender trust. If the open palms face downwards or back, this signals a desire to control the situation or the other person's responses. Frequent gestures indicate excitement and generally mean the person is not actively controlling their hands.

Heads are tricky because head movements are largely controlled and can have culturally significant variations. In the west, a shake of the head is a no and, done unconsciously, suggests doubt or denial. But in Southeast Asia, a similar gesture can mean agreement. So, for nods, shakes and tilts of the head, you will be safest if you interpret them according to the culture in which the person grew up. However, a head tip, lowering the chin to the upper chest, often signifies a moment of accessing a deep feeling, although figuring out what that feeling is won't always be possible. And it could be empathy for someone else in the room.

Lastly, let's talk about everybody's favourite: eye contact. Again, there are cultural variations and the absolute times will differ from person to person. But steady eye contact suggests either confidence and openness, or deliberate control (which may mean exactly the opposite!). Avoiding eye contact can likewise suggest nervousness or evasion, but it may also be the way that person is – some people find eye contact uncomfortable. However, I think we can be confident that excessive staring is a deliberate act. It usually signifies an attempt to dominate and may therefore be aggressive. However, you may just have food on your face, and they are staring at that!

How you speak

On the boundary between spoken communication and body language is the way you use your voice, as opposed to what you say. This covers things like tone, pace, rhythm, inflection and volume.

For most of us, and for most of the time, this is something we don't bother to even try to control. But for expert communicators, these are all individual levers to control, which can convey precise nuance or powerful emotion.

However, it is the other side of the coin that interests us most as negotiators. Our inflection and pace can betray our emotions. If we cannot keep them in check, then perhaps we need control our speech, so we do not wholly give our emotions away.

The easiest aspect of our speech to control is pace. Deliberately slow down to give your words more impact, and speed it up to convey energy and excitement. If you are not yet able to slow down as much as you would like, short pauses give the impression of slow, deliberate phrases, and allow you to punctuate your comments to drive home a point.

Use of language in spoken communication

Whilst beautifully crafted language can win a debate and enchant a reader or theatre audience, in the world of business communication, two things matter more than anything: clarity and precision:

Clarity: to what extent can people understand what you say in the same way as you intended?

Precision: to what extent do you say exactly what you mean – and mean exactly what you say?

These are important in negotiation because each party will make judgments and, ultimately, form an agreement based on the words each party uses. One misunderstanding can act like the centre of a snowball. Rolling down the hill, it can accumulate layer upon layer of misinterpretation, all based on that one error.

And whose error was it? A good communicator and negotiator will always take responsibility for the words they use and how they use them. 'If you misunderstand me,' they will believe, 'then I was at fault.' This means you need not only to speak with care, but you must also pay particular attention to how your words land. Look for clues in the body language of their response. And then assess whether their next words suggest they did understand because, if they did not, you need to put it right immediately.

This is why you may be better to speak less than you want to and listen more than they expect. As we will see in the next section, listening is the real talent in spoken communication.

A good communicator and negotiator will also take responsibility for understanding what the other party has said. And yes, this *is* unfair – they take responsibility for both sides of the conversation because it matters to them to get communication right. Here's another reason why listening is so important.

If you are not completely satisfied that you understand what you hear, ask questions to clarify uncertainty and test your interpretation. Each time you confirm that both sides share a common

Figure 9.1   Taking responsibility for your communication

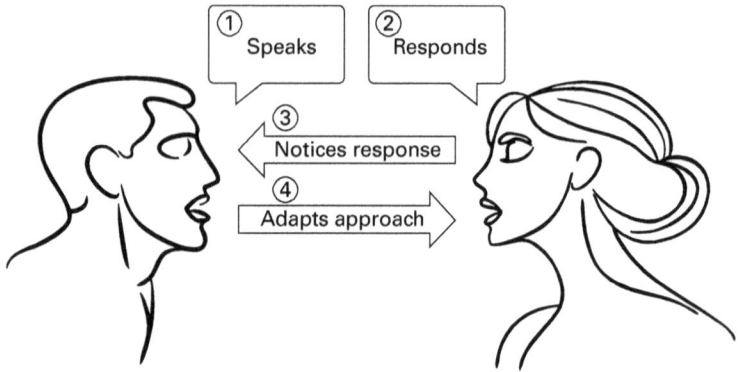

understanding, you create a stable platform for the next part of the conversation. If you don't do this, each platform may be just a little loose or slightly off true. Eventually the structure of your negotiation could topple and fall.

Top tips

What are the tips for good communication that is clear and precise?

- Make use of pauses to think about what you are going to say, and how you are going to say it, before you speak.
- Use simple words that a young child could understand.
- Use plain language to describe things. Avoid jargon, unless you are certain that both parties share a common understanding of the term and a strong familiarity with it. If you must use jargon, explain it clearly.
- Keep sentence structures simple. Ideally, allow one idea per sentence.
- If you need to convey a number of points, signpost this fact, and count off the points as you go.

- State things as positives. Our brains need to work twice as hard to unscramble the meaning of a negative statement. Double negatives are worse. Double negatives are not better. Don't avoid using positive language. (Can you see what I mean?)
- Use numbers to quantify things. A few, a lot, small and big convey ideas but not precision.
- Metaphors and analogies help people understand complex ideas. Be careful to keep them within the realm of applicability. They are not precise.

Listening

There is a difference between hearing and listening. Hearing is a physiological function but listening is a deliberate choice. A lot of the time, our listening is shallow. We pay attention to any number of things as well as what the other person is saying, and make use of our brain's ability to spot something important when we hear it.

This triggers the 'hold on a moment' reflex as we try to track back through our short-term memory to replay the last few words, in the hope of catching what was important. That replay function is called the phonological loop and it only lasts a few seconds. So, sometimes, we miss what we should have heard. This kind of selective listening is not appropriate for a negotiation. And neither is it respectful to the person we are pretending to listen to!

Active listening allows us to interpret what we have heard, understand the other person's point of view and build their trust. The craft of active listening combines several essential skills:

- being curious about what the other person knows, thinks and feels, so you can better understand their point of view;
- turning off the voice in your head that wants to comment on what you are hearing, or talk about things outside of the negotiation entirely;

- putting your own point of view out of the way and allowing yourself to absorb the other person's point of view;
- refraining from trying to plan your response, rebuttal or next question while they are speaking;
- using your body language, gestures and vocalizations to encourage the other person to keep speaking, without interrupting their flow;
- other than these signals, keeping still so you don't distract the other person;
- remaining silent after they stop speaking, to give them time to add more if they want to. This also gives you time to turn your attention to your own response or next question.

People want to be heard, so there is nothing you can do that is more respectful than to set everything else aside to listen to them.

Questioning

If you want answers, ask questions.

If you want good answers, ask good questions.

Questions are not as confrontational as statements. Yet they can lead to the same insight – often more quickly. If I tell you something, you have to be prepared to believe I am right. If I ask you, and you give an answer, you'll believe that straight away, because it is *your* answer. You can use questions to control the direction of a conversation and drop ideas and insights into the other person's mind.

And, of course, questions are the way we learn what someone else wants, believes, knows, thinks or feels. They are how we gather data, elicit information and clarify our understanding of a situation. So, how do we ask the good questions that will get the answers we need both effectively and efficiently? The answer to that starts with a funnel.

Figure 9.2 Questioning funnel

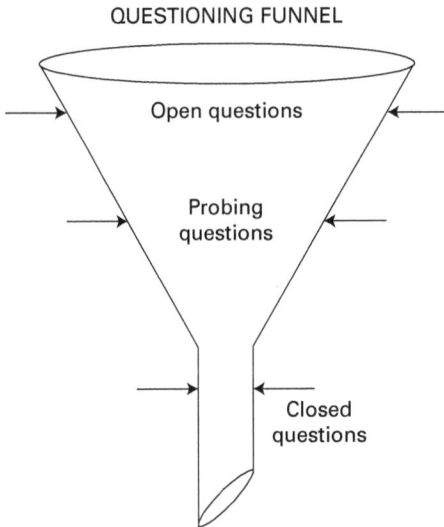

The questioning funnel starts with the wide, open end and tapers down to the narrow end, where we can ask what are called 'closed' questions that limit the range of answers that are possible.

Open questions

We start the questioning process with an 'open question'. This type of question makes no constraint on how it can be answered. It is a great way to get a broad overview of the topic you want to cover before you narrow the questions to the areas you want to concentrate on in detail. They demonstrate that you are interested to hear the other person's point of view and allow them to express themselves as they choose.

Open questions often start with 'what' or 'how'. A 'what' question allows them to select what they want to focus on. Often, a 'how' question will follow and focus them on action. But by asking it, you show that you want them to collaborate in finding a solution that will satisfy them.

A question starting with 'why' is also an open question. But it is wise to avoid 'why' questions because they focus the responder on their reasons and values. This can feel, to them, like a challenge to their reasoning and values. Asking 'why?' can evoke a defensive response that does not provide useful information. At its worst, it can be perceived as rude and damage a relationship. If you want to know why, then try an alternative question that gets you to the answer you need, with less chance of causing defensiveness of giving offence. Ask something like, 'What was the reason for...' or 'When you did that, what was your priority?'

Open questions don't even need to be structured as a question. If you start with 'Tell me about...', it works like a wide-open question that could be a what, how and why question all rolled into one!

Probing questions

When your open questions have charted the territory, it's time to narrow your exploration down to the areas that interest you. For this, we use probing questions. You can use these to either elicit more detailed information or to further focus the direction of the negotiation and we do that with probing questions. Examples of probing questions include:

'How would this work?'

'What in particular is important to you about this?'

'Tell me more about...'

Probing questions take the conversation along a direction. Sometimes, when you have learned what you need to, you will want to come back to the answer you got from your open questions and then probe in a new direction.

One particularly useful form of probing question in the context of a negotiation is the 'what if' question. This is the way you can explore different scenarios, contingencies and hypotheticals. For this reason, 'what if' is an example of a hypothetical question.

There are other ways to ask hypothetical questions. For example:

'If we were to make this concession, what would you be able to offer in return?'

'Suppose we needed this extra consideration; how would we deal with it?'

'If we asked for this by March, what would your response be?'

'What if we agreed this?'

Hypothetical questions like 'what if' encourage exploration of different solutions and are a great way to start a trial close.

Probing questions give you a lot of detailed information. But sometimes you want to be clear that you have understood something correctly. Now is the time for the third type of question in our funnel, the 'closed question'. There is little scope for the answer to be in any format other than the one the question implies – hence its name. This type of question gives you certainty.

Closed questions

The commonest form of closed question evokes a yes/no answer. For example, 'Here's what I think you want… Have I got this right?' The question part of this will get a yes or a no. Or maybe not. Don't try to use these manipulatively to force a yes or no. It is perfectly reasonable for the answer to be 'sort of' or 'in parts'. Now you can refine your understanding by asking more probing questions.

One specific type of closed question is designed to elicit either the answer 'yes' or the answer 'no'. This is not an enquiring yes/no question where you don't know the answer and you want to clarify. Rather, your aim is to get a yes or to get a no. We'll cover that in Chapter 12, Traps.

Not all closed questions have a yes or no answer. 'When do you need it?' is a closed question because it directs the response to be a specific date or time. So too are questions beginning 'where' or 'who'.

Risky questions

In addition to open, probing and closed questions, there are two other types of questions. You need to be aware of them because each carries risk.

Leading questions are questions that presuppose one particular answer. They are a way to try to manipulate the other person into giving you a response that you want. This may sound like a great tactic, but consider that if they don't spot it at the time, they may later. And even if they do not, they may end up making an agreement that they later regret. If they do spot the manipulation, they won't like it. Whatever way, the outcome is a loss of trust and a damaged relationship.

Multiple questions pose more than one question in the form of a single question. For example, 'Would you be prepared to make this concession and then, if you do, what would you want in return, and how soon can you implement the ideas?' This may seem like an efficient way to get through business, but it can cause confusion and may result in one or more parts of the multiple question getting overlooked and therefore remaining unanswered.

Maybe 'don't use multiple questions' is a bit strong, but do avoid them if you can. There will always be a way to separate them out and maintain control of the question flow, by asking individual questions. For example, 'I have three questions, and my first one is…'.

Empathic negotiation

Communication is about conveying information and building a relationship. We've focused on the information-sharing aspect, so let's consider what to focus on to build rapport and create empathy.

While the other person is speaking, show that you are listening and value what you are hearing. Nodding, using tag words like 'aha' or 'I see', and taking notes will convey your attention and interest. They can also start to show your understanding.

If you want to emphasize your understanding, then your response should restate, in summary, what they have said. Critically, reuse some of the key words they used. If you restate their comment using different words, you run the risk of them thinking, 'That's not what I said'. To you, your word means the same as theirs, but to them, the subtle nuances of meaning may make for a significant difference that matters very much. If you aren't sure what they meant by a word or phrase, you can clarify by either asking a question or rephrasing it and asking if that is what they mean.

If you want to emphasize your understanding, use phrases like these to build rapport:

'I understand that…'

'I can see that you think that…'

'I appreciate why you're saying…'

You don't need to be told that interruptions can break rapport at best and seem rude at worst. But even responding when the other person stops speaking can break rapport if you do it too quickly. It will feel like you have just been waiting to have your say and maybe have not been listening. If you had, you'd need a moment to decide how to respond. So, pause before you respond.

In this pause, you can reflect on what you have heard and review what you want to say. This gift of silence tells the other person that what they said is important to you, so you need to think about it. And there's another aspect of silence that is worth knowing:

In a negotiation, the person who is more comfortable with silence has an advantage.

People don't like silence and they will try to fill it. If you leave a silence after the other person has stopped talking, they may fill it with something they had not planned to say. And this could be useful. If they ask for a concession and you wait before answering, they might feel embarrassed and withdraw their request, or maybe reduce what they asked for.

Either way, diving in with a quick, preplanned response leaves the impression that their question was obvious, or their point was simplistic. There's a chance that, by not considering what you say, you'll get it wrong. And a fast response shows a complete lack of empathy for the other person.

When you do respond, you need to take responsibility for your opinions and feelings, by using the words 'me', 'my' and 'I'. For example:

'I think that...'

'I feel that...'

'My assessment is that...'

These make it clear that it is your perception, and that you aren't trying to put *your* words into *their* mouth. On the other hand, if you say something like 'you said', and then recast their words into what you wish they had said, you are manipulating them. This is not high-integrity negotiating, and it will break empathy.

If you need to, you can soften your response by saying something like, 'I'm sorry that...'. Do note, however, that it is important to use 'I'm sorry that...' rather than 'I'm sorry but...'. As soon as we hear the word 'but', we immediately forget what came before it, including the apology. 'I'm sorry that' signals that you're going to say something that might be challenging to them and prepares them for it.

After you have disagreed, you need to refocus the conversation on solutions and ways forward. Let them know that this is what you want to do with an opening like:

'I have a question...'

'There's something I'd like to add to...'

'Can I propose an alternative...'

'I'd like to make a suggestion...'

Now they know what is coming, so you can maintain rapport despite a shift in the direction of the conversation. This will make the transition into your preference a little bit smoother. You will build a better understanding of each other and strengthen the relationship on which a negotiated agreement depends.

Summary points

- First impressions matter. So be deliberate in how you come across on first meeting someone.

- Your appearance is made up of what you look like, how you dress and your body language.

- Reading the body language of the other party can give you insights into their state of mind and maybe some of their thoughts.

- A good read of body language needs a baseline, a cluster of observations and an understanding of context. Even then, there can be multiple interpretations of what you observe.

- Another important signal we give out is the way we speak: our tone, pace, rhythm, volume and inflection of speech.

- In negotiation, spoken language needs to be clear and precise.

- Listening is vital. It needs to be active and deliberate.

- Good questions get good answers and can also direct the flow of the negotiation and the ideas that emerge.

- Your main questions should form a funnel of open, then probing, then closed questions. Be careful with leading and multiple questions.

- Build empathy with signals of your understanding, pauses and silence, and taking responsibility for your opinions and feelings.

10
Influence

Influence is like a nudge: persuasion is more of a push

The subject of influence is a huge one and, without a doubt, it is highly relevant for a negotiator. Getting the agreement that you want is, in large part, about influencing the other party to make the concessions you need and accept terms that will suit you.

In this chapter, we will look at the key elements of influence and persuasion, and focus on the methods that are most useful in the type of day-to-day workplace negotiations that this book is about.

These methods can be powerful. However, they are not magical – you cannot always flip someone's opinion with some clever words, despite what some movies may suggest. When they work, it is because they combine a strong argument with well-chosen psychological insights to deliver a compelling case. However, just as we have been focusing on negotiating with integrity, you also need to influence and persuade with integrity. This means that you must not use techniques in a manipulative or coercive way.

We'll start by introducing five important elements of influence, and then look at some of the simple methods you can apply within each to bring them to life.

The five elements of influence

The five elements of influence that will serve you well as a negotiator are:

1 Establishing your character: before anyone will listen to you, they have to be prepared to listen to *you*.

2 Making your argument: giving the reasons why someone should believe as you do or do as you want them to.

3 Refuting objections: handling counterarguments and resistance to complying with your wishes.

4 Appealing to emotion: because people don't make decisions based on reason, but on the way they feel.

5 Intelligent persistence: having the commitment to keep trying in the face of a no, but not to the point of foolishness.

In the remaining sections of this chapter, we'll see why each element is important, and look at three important ideas for how you can apply your influence.

Establishing your character

Why should the other party pay attention to what you have to say? The answer will be because of who you are and what you bring to the meeting. Therefore, before any negotiation begins, you need to establish your character because people start with their gut instinct. This is why the opening step of the negotiation is critical.

Character is about how we behave in different situations, especially those that challenge us. It leads to liking, respect and trust. We often assess these things through observations of two characteristics: attitudes and actions.

Character shows in the attitudes we have towards people and situations. There may be a level of cultural variation and you will certainly have your own priorities, but some of the attitudes that demonstrate good character in a negotiator are respect for others, keenness to listen, flexibility, a willingness to embrace uncertainty, preparedness to work hard and a desire to be led by evidence and reason.

Actions speak louder than words or, as Henry Ford said:

You can't build a reputation on what you are going to do.

Attitudes are important, but they only matter when they are backed up by a record of consistent actions.

Establishing your character idea number 1 is credibility. Early on, you need to set out why you are a credible counterparty to the negotiation. This will come from a combination of your position and authority, your expertise and mastery of the situation, and your qualifications and track record. This does not mean bragging about your achievements and making a show of your status. But it does require you to establish that you have earned your place in the conversation. When someone has both positional and intellectual authority, we are willing to listen to them and consider what they have to say.

Establishing your character idea number 2 is trust. People want to negotiate with someone they trust, and credibility is only one element of that. Other elements are how much they:

- like you and feel you have empathy for them and their concerns;
- have confidence that you will keep your word and do what you say you will;
- believe you are the person you portray yourself to be, that you are authentic;
- assess your motives as selfless, rather than driven by selfish desires.

This list gives you four more things to work on to build real trust in you as a person.

Establishing your character idea number 3 is similarity. Put simply, we like and trust people that we think are like us. Humans are tribal creatures. But we live simultaneously in many tribes. So, your task is to find a big enough area of overlap between yourself and the other person for them to feel that you and they have something important in common. For example, it might be an experience, an interest or an allegiance. The more the other party feels you and they can identify with one another, the more they will like, respect and trust you, for one simple reason: they are effectively liking, respecting and trusting themselves!

Making your argument

The core of any attempt to influence is a reasoned argument that marshals the evidence into a logical structure. Facts alone can never persuade. But, without them, all other forms of influence are merely manipulation. So, you need to appeal to the other party's rational mind.

But, under the heading of 'appealing to emotion', below, you will read that nobody ever makes a decision based on the facts. So why do facts matter? Why can you not just make an emotive case, devoid of any form of reasoning?

Whether the reasoning is sound or not (and you aren't playing a political game, so it needs to be), you need to provide it for one of two reasons. People may make their decisions for emotional reasons, but they absolutely need a set of reasons to:

- justify their decision to the people around them and to whom they are accountable; or
- justify their decision to themselves.

Making your argument idea number 1 is answering the 'why?' This follows closely from the need for justification. Just like small children, adults hear the question 'why?' in their heads as soon as they are asked to accept or do something they don't understand, don't believe or don't want. And, unless they get a nice, juicy 'because' to answer that question, they will never be motivated to accept, believe or do that thing. They may, of course, feel they have no choice, which can happen in the workplace. But they won't feel good about it. Explaining your position or a request in a nego-tiation by using the word 'because', signposts that there is a good reason, and that they can use it to justify a 'yes'. Likewise, always attach a 'because' statement to any disagreement or negative re-sponse to a request.

Making your argument idea number 2 is cognitive dissonance. Cognitive dissonance is the discomfort we feel when we try to hold two conflicting beliefs together. As an example, you have a lot of things that you want to do, but you also want to spend the day with a group of friends. A good way to use this in the negotiating context is to make a note of anything the other party says that could be helpful in making your own arguments. This can include actions they have taken in the past, policies their organization has or previous commitments. You can then use their words, or something similar, later. When we commit to something, especially in front of other people, we feel compelled to make choices that are consistent with it because, if our decisions conflict, it can cause cognitive dissonance and maybe even cause us to lose face.

Making your argument idea number 3 is social proof. Other people have a shockingly big impact on our thinking. The success of testimonials, endorsements and case studies in marketing and sales is evidence of that. So, a way to strengthen your case is to cite other people, particularly authority figures the other party will respect, who have supported or will support your argument.

Refuting objections

No matter how good your case is, there is always the possibility of objections. People resist ideas for many reasons, so your first task is to learn what the source of their resistance is.

It could be as simple as their not understanding what you are saying. Or maybe they understand you, but are not clear why you are saying it. They may have concerns about your credibility or motives, or simply can't make the connections they need to make. It might be that they don't like what you are saying, or they might object because they simply don't like the feeling of being told. Or, perhaps, it's not your ideas they are really objecting to; it might be you!

Before looking at our three ideas, we can also use the idea of cognitive dissonance to handle objections. If you can point out a way that their resistance is contrary to a position they have taken earlier, or conflicts with past actions or existing policies, then you can trigger cognitive dissonance. But please don't do this in a way that might shame or belittle them by suggesting they shouldn't have said or done something in the past. This will break rapport and therefore trust.

Refuting objections idea number 1 is slicing the pie. Whatever the objection is, narrow it down to as small a part of the whole pie as you can. It is easier to overcome resistance to a small thing than a big thing and if you can show that they agree on most of the issues, it frames the objection as a matter of detail. It also means that it will be easier to search for solutions where you have a specific problem to focus on.

Refuting objections idea number 2 is exchanging offers and concessions. Humans are wired to expect fairness. Any imbalance feels acutely unfair to us. This is why trading concessions, offers and compromises works. If you cannot get past an objection, go around it or over it with a concession or a compromise. We can see the process of negotiation as one of give and take, this-for-that or reciprocity. If you reject something, I can make another offer or grant a concession. We build agreement one trade at a time.

Refuting objections idea number 3 is being specific in your offers and requests. The other party will feel much safer in accepting an offer or granting a concession if they are clear what it is. If there is some doubt or it feels in some way open-ended, this will introduce uncertainty and they may reject the risk of possibly allowing themselves to walk into a trap. This will take longer, but building agreement in small, precise, structured stages offers more certainty.

Appealing to emotion

An earlier section foreshadowed the assertion that nobody ever makes a decision based on the facts. And this is true. We do what we want to do and decide what we want to decide. So, decisions are based on our emotional responses. 'Hold on,' you say, 'I do things I don't want to do.' So you do. But why do you do those things? You do them out of duty, loyalty or obligation. And what are these? Emotions.

As we'll see below, in a negotiation, we use words to conjure emotions. One critical influencing word for negotiators that we have already seen is 'because', but that is more about reason than emotion. There is one word that can really make people feel good, however: their name. Use people's names, but don't overuse them like an unskilled shop salesperson.

Whatever you do, use names properly. Don't use an abbreviated form if the person doesn't introduce them that way. If they call themselves Christina or Christopher, do not call them Chris. But if I introduce myself as Mike, then that's what I expect you to use: not Mick, Mikey and certainly not Michael. Only my parents use that – and the Inland Revenue! And we live in a multicultural society. This means you will meet people whose names are unfamiliar. Listen to how they pronounce their name. If you only see it written, ask. Nobody is offended if you take an interest and show them the courtesy of pronouncing the name correctly. Lazily getting it wrong is likely to cause offence – and rightly so.

Appealing to emotion idea number 1 is making them feel good. And, equally important, avoid any temptation to throw shade and make them feel bad. This is key because the outcome of your negotiation is more important to you than who gets the credit for the success. So, it's fine to be generous with the credit for any ideas, suggestions or proposals that work. Okay, it might have been your idea, but who cares? Getting the agreement is what matters, not feeling good about your contributions. So, let other people take the credit for your ideas, do it willingly and even encourage it. Your pride is not the prize: the agreement is.

Appealing to emotion idea number 2 is storytelling. Humans have evolved to be storytelling creatures. We love to tell and hear stories. Stories have characters, events, lessons and, critically, emotions. They are therefore a great way to introduce an emotional component to an otherwise objective workplace negotiation. We tell stories when we share experiences and anecdotes, draw analogies and use metaphors or similes. They are a way to move the conversation from the abstract to the real. This makes it easier for people to understand the ideas and empathize with the outcomes.

Appealing to emotion idea number 3 is me and you. Pronouns matter. When we use words like the first person I and me, or the second person you and your, we can impact the tone of a conversation. Both first- and second-person pronouns have a light and dark side. Choosing the right one makes a difference.

Let's start with you (which is always better than starting with me). When I talk about what *you* want and what the negotiation means for *you*, this is the light side. It suggests my focus is on your priorities. If I use the 'you' pronoun properly, it tells you that I care about *you*, that *you* are important to me and that I recognize *your* interests in this negotiation.

But, if I don't like what you said and talk about what *you* think or what *you're* telling me in an accusatory way, saying something like 'you said this', or 'you want everything', this can destroy our rapport.

The light and dark side of the personal pronouns I and me are similar. If I talk about what *I* want and what the negotiation needs to give *me*, that can come across as self-oriented and damage trust. But if I talk about how *I* feel about what you said, or why *I* don't like this offer, it shows me taking responsibility for *my* feelings or *my* assessment.

Intelligent persistence

Negotiation can be a long process. To succeed in negotiation or persuasion, you need to be resilient to setbacks and prepared to persist to get what you want. One approach is known as the 'broken record' approach. Old vinyl records could pick up a scratch and repeat the same loop of music again and again. This is a persuasion tactic beloved of small children!

And it works. Salespeople know that you need to keep coming back, in the knowledge that each rejection may be one more step towards an agreement. 'Seven times' is often cited. I have never seen any supporting evidence for this, but there will come a time when it just feels like you are banging against a locked door. And maybe the door *is* locked. Intelligent persistence is marked by a willingness to constantly re-evaluate the signals you are getting, and to disengage as soon as it becomes clear that no amount of effort will successfully persuade.

However, until this point, stick with it. Stay calm, stay respectful and keep trying different approaches. If you keep the same approach, you may wear them down, but a better approach is:

If at first you don't succeed, try, try something else.

Intelligent persistence idea number 1 is that, to move the mind, first move the body. Mind and body are connected. In martial arts, shifting someone's attention is a way to change their posture. So, if you can move somebody's body, you may just give their mind the nudge it needs to make a shift. This is what one former colleague described as 'walking someone around the car park'. And that is exactly what he would do. If your negotiation stalls, get everyone up from the table and move around. Maybe even change venue.

Intelligent persistence idea number 2 is allowing them to save face. Sometimes people get stuck in a rut. They are so used to disagreeing that, when they realize they should really agree, they can't bring themselves to. This is another example of cognitive dissonance, which we saw above. They believe they are seen as someone who is right, yet they weren't right. The only way to stop the discomfort is to close their mind off from the possibility that they were wrong.

Changing their mind would cause them to lose face. People don't like to do that. But we also noted that it doesn't matter who gets the credit for what, if the final agreement is a good one. So, why don't you take some unwarranted blame, to help them change their mind?

The 'one more piece of information' approach can save them the embarrassment of being seen to change their mind. You might say something like, 'Oh! I just realized that there's one thing I might have forgotten to tell you, and this may help you make a decision.' Now they have a reason to pass the blame onto you and say, 'If only you told me that earlier. This changes everything!' If there is a small snippet of information, no matter how inconsequential, use it. But if there isn't, then use something you know you've already told them, but pretend you have forgotten that you told them about it. It doesn't matter what it is. This is their backdoor to escape from a decision that they don't want to have to make and save face at the same time.

Intelligent persistence idea number 3 is gentle pressure. At some point, you may want to exert a little gentle pressure. This is tricky, because there is a fine line between pushing gently and coercion. But it is possible to do this with integrity. Deadlines are a good example. Creating a fake deadline to create urgency is manipulative. But noting when you are approaching a real deadline is reasonable. If you are negotiating about a finite resource like materials or people's time, it is a mean tactic to limit availability to apply pressure, but wholly appropriate to be clear what real limitations are present.

But wait... there's more!

If you can offer a small – even miniscule – extra benefit at the end of a negotiation, this can have a profound impact on willingness to agree. Advertisers reckon this kind of 'add-on' can create a significant shift in the uptake of an offer. It may well also work for you.

Summary points

- The techniques of influence are powerful – but not magical. They can work well, but won't always work.
- The five elements of influence are character, reason, refutation, emotion and persistence.
- Character is about integrity, credibility, liking, attitude and actions.

- You can build trust with credibility, empathy, reliability, authenticity and selflessness.

- We like and trust people who are like ourselves.

- People use rational arguments to justify the decisions they make, so you need to answer the question 'why?'

- We need to feel that our words and choices align. If they don't, we feel a discomfort called cognitive dissonance.

- We trust the judgments of other people we respect.

- If the other party resists or objects, first discover why.

- Minimize the scale of the disagreement by being precise about where the objection is.

- When you need to trade offers and concessions to make progress, be very specific with them.

- We make decisions based on our emotional response to the situation, and justify them with reasons.

- Using people's names correctly, and often, feels good to them.

- Be generous in giving credit for progress. The outcome is worth more than the kudos.

- Use stories to inject emotion into abstract ideas.

- Make careful choices about when to use 'I' or 'me', and when to use 'you' or 'your'.

- Persistence can unlock results. But know when to stop.

- Physical movement can move a negotiation forward.

- Help the other party save face if they feel uncomfortable or embarrassed to change their mind.

- If you need to, apply gentle pressure in an ethical way.

11
Psychology

Psychology teaches us how people think and make choices

Of all the things a manager or professional can learn about, psychology is, arguably, the most useful. This is particularly the case when thinking about effective negotiation. You need to understand both the psychology of the other person and your own psychology.

It's tempting to see this as two subjects but, of course, they are not. You and the other person have very similar emotional and physiological responses to things that go on. It's like you are mirrors of one another. So, you can interpret the sections below as being about you or about the other people in the room.

This section tackles four topics from the world of psychology that are particularly valuable to negotiators. Please take these as a starting point for learning more about psychology and how understanding more about it can make you an even better negotiator.

Understanding responses

Everything that happens in our environment will trigger a response. In a negotiation, this can give away what we are thinking and potentially cause conflict or offence. So, we need to be able to avoid letting our emotions take control. Learning to manage your emotions is critical to your success, and it starts with your ability to understand how you are feeling.

This emotional awareness is a prerequisite for taking control of disruptive emotional responses and impulses. You need to avoid showing frustration or impatience, becoming upset or angry, feeling the need to retaliate or inflict harm, or walking out because of these emotions. You must learn how to:

1 spot the signs in your body that your emotional responses have been activated;

2 recognize the things that trigger you to respond emotionally;

3 take control and rein in your emotional responses.

This is the best way to stop high levels of emotions from disrupting a negotiation.

Certainly, expressing impatience, frustration, disappointment or anger is a reasonable thing to do. But you must do it in a controlled way. Walking away from a potential conflict can be the right thing to do. But if you are going to make a display move like this, do it calmly and in a considered way, and only as a last resort when other, more collaborative approaches have failed.

One of the most important triggers to understand is reactance. This is the need we feel to resist and push back against a choice that we perceive someone to be imposing upon us. When someone threatens to take something away from us, we react by trying harder to maintain control of it. If they pressure you to do something, you will want to do anything but that thing.

This means that anything that seems to limit our freedom can trigger reactance. But that is the nature of negotiation, which is about asking the other side to make choices. You need to spot a reactance response in yourself and interrogate it. How can you better evaluate what is in front of you and consider your options with objectivity? Likewise, it is helpful to anticipate how the other party might perceive your proposals, offers or requests, and find a way that minimizes the likelihood of reactance.

There are three other factors that can strongly affect how you or they will respond to a negotiating position: anchoring, priming and framing.

The anchoring effect is a subconscious bias where a piece of information or a number that we have become aware of can affect subsequent choices we make. This is something you can use in the opening step of a negotiation – either when stating your position, or in earlier conversation. Equally, something you have seen or heard early on can influence your own reaction to the negotiation, without your conscious awareness of it.

Priming is similar, but works more at the physiological level. A stimulus, like a statement, a prop or a visual aid, can influence people's response to what comes next. This can be very subtle, and it is not something you should be using as a negotiating tactic. However, this effect can impact your own responses. Even something as simple as seeing an emotive image in the news before starting work can result in a different response in you.

How you present information can affect decision-making in another person. This is framing. An example of this is whether something is shown as a loss or a gain. Since we have a cognitive bias to avoid loss, you can frame two alternative options either as:

- Option A is a base option, but for an additional payment, you can get the enhanced Option B.
- Option C is the full option, but for a reduction in payment, you could get the basic Option D.

Here, the loss aversion bias would more often lead to the selection of the cheaper Option A in the first example. However, in the second example, the fear of losing something valuable from the full package would more often lead to the more expensive Option C. So, how you frame the base option – as either the full package or the minimum package – can affect the choice that is made, even when the cost and benefit differentials are identical.

The role of empathy in negotiation

Empathy is the ability to understand another person's feelings, thoughts and experiences. It is the basis of building a rapport, and an important part of leading, motivating and influencing. In most people, empathy is a natural capability that allows us to make emotional connections with the people around us.

If you hone your empathic abilities, you can become more attuned to the particular feelings and ways of thinking of other people. This has two powerful consequences in negotiation. First is the ability to read the room and assess how other people are responding to something that has happened or been said. Second, you can use your empathy for someone to hone your influencing of them.

It can also have problematic consequences. Emotions can be contagious. In a group, one person's strong emotions can affect the emotional state of others around them. This can influence group dynamics. If you are in a leadership role, people may disproportionately take their emotional cues from you. This makes it doubly important to control your emotional responses. To maintain a collaborative and optimistic mood in the room, you must remain positive and optimistic.

There is compelling evidence that this kind of empathic reciprocation is mediated by a set of brain cells called mirror neurons. A mirror neuron fires when we make a movement, gesture or expression, and when we observe the same action performed by another person. It's what allows us, if we concentrate, to interpret the meaning and feelings behind an expression or gesture.

At a low level, you can use this effect to your advantage – as can others with you. For example, if you want someone to agree with you, just smile, nod and maintain eye contact while you're talking. They will be likely to nod back.

We can adapt this into the verbal domain. When the other person has made an important point, repeat the key words back to them. They will subconsciously get the feeling that you have understood them and are a great listener. Just don't paraphrase too far and risk shifting the meaning. If you can summarize what they have said, and what they want you to know, and then look at them and pause, they may confirm by saying 'that's right'. You'll know from this that you have made real progress.

The mirroring of emotional responses has two consequences to be extremely wary of: projection and transference. These psychological terms describe what can often happen in a negotiation.

Projection is a psychological defence mechanism where we unconsciously attribute our own thoughts, feelings or reactions onto someone else. I get angry, but don't want to take responsibility for my own anger, so I project it onto you and tell you not to get angry. Now I have a reason to feel anger and I can blame it on you!

Transference happens when someone redirects their feelings about one person onto someone else. For example, I might see my negotiating counterpart as being in some way like someone I knew in the past. I might transfer my feelings towards that person and my interpretations of their motives, for example, onto the person I am with now.

Transference is a good reason for avoiding gossip. The term 'spontaneous trait transference' describes what happens when people think of you as having the traits that you describe in someone else. So, for example, if you hear me deprecating a colleague for their lack of energy, you might spontaneously transfer that trait to me and unconsciously think of me as lacking energy. On the other hand, if you only say good things about people (as your mother doubtless advised you), then that attitude might positively affect people's perception of you.

Power

In psychology and negotiation, power is the ability to decide, influence or control a situation. And all power in a negotiating context is social power – that is, the power we hold by virtue of our social relationships. Psychologists John French and Bertram Raven introduced the term 'power bases' to describe the different sources of social power we can hold.

There are different articulations of the power bases, but it makes sense to start with a distinction between the power we hold because of who we are and that we hold because of some aspect of what we have or the position we hold. Both are relevant to a negotiation.

Positional power

Positional power bases in a negotiation come from status and what that status gives us access to. Importantly, positional power is usually in someone else's gift. And that means someone can always take it away. Let's start with the power people have that flows directly from their position; the authority, status and influence that comes from a place in a hierarchy. The more senior you are, the greater your hierarchical power.

With this often comes two other forms of power, which are like opposite sides of a coin. These are power bases that we need to be very careful with in the context of a negotiation, because they are the power to offer inducements (reward power) or threats (coercive power).

There is one other form of power that comes with a particular position. This is called resource power, and it is based on an ability to control access to something someone else wants. It is the power any gatekeeper has, from a personal assistant guarding their boss's time, to a storekeeper who controls access to supplies, or a banking executive who decides on loan requests. The lead negotiators on each side of a negotiation both have resource power.

Personal power

The other forms of power are more to do with who you are and what you can do. Information power, for example, could be a form of resource power if you have access to information that other people want. But if you have this information in your head, then it is yours. This makes it a form of personal power that nobody can remove.

Expert power is related to this but different. I can share with you a whole lot of facts, data and other information. But how well can you put it to use? This ability is the power of expertise. And while information can quickly become outdated, expertise lasts longer and can be applied to new data in new situations.

It is not just what you know that gives you personal power, it is also who you know. Connection power is the power you have from the ability to mobilize support and assistance from other people. It is also their willingness to stand behind you and make you stronger.

But why would people do that? It is not enough to have a network with a lot of names in your address book. True connection power comes from the quality as well as the quantity of relationships. And this is driven literally by who you are; the person you choose to be. It is perhaps best known as personal power, the power of your personality, likeability, integrity and character. It is why people like, respect and support you.

However, we can also include the authority of expertise, the credibility of deep knowledge and the web of supportive connections under the umbrella term of 'personal power'. This is why French and Raven introduced a new term, 'referent power'. This is the intrinsic 'power' of the person to whom you are referring. Unfortunately, this term causes a lot of confusion and is misdescribed in a number of books. Maybe 'immediate personal power' is less confusing.

Whatever power bases you have, it pays to use your power with caution. Indeed, only step it up as and when it is the only way to achieve what you legitimately need to achieve. After all, the quote from the Spider-Man comics has become as popular and widely known as it has because it is true:

With great power comes great responsibility.

Positions around the table

Have you ever noticed that, going into a meeting, there is often a little ritual of deciding where to sit? It should be no surprise that there is some subtle psychology behind how it feels to sit in different spots around a meeting room table.

One-on-one negotiation

Let's start with the simplest case: a one-on-one negotiation between two people around one table. How hard can that be?

You can understand what is going on, as soon as you recognize that there are three factors to consider:

- position
- distance
- alignment

Position is about where you sit in the room. Typically, if there is a window, simple architectural rules suggest it is most likely to be opposite the door. The power position – and therefore the one you probably want to adopt – is the one facing the door. This also usually puts your back to the window. Because someone can come in at any time, having your back to the door is a little unsettling. And facing the window can be distracting. Having your back to the window is better, not just because you don't have the distraction, but because the sun may make a seat opposite just a little uncomfortable. If the door is not opposite the window, then both parties may be oblique to the window.

You may choose not to take the small psychological advantage position could give you. You might change the alignment of seats or even deliberately take the other position, to grant the power position to your colleague. However, initiating this generosity (reward power) is as much a statement of power as enforcing an advantage (coercive power).

The next thing to consider is the degree of alignment or opposition of you and your negotiating partner. The more completely your directions are aligned, the more it represents agreement and cooperation. The more opposite your alignment, the more adversarial you will feel, making agreement harder and signifying (perhaps even leading to) conflict.

A useful tip is that if you fear the other person will be angry or adversarial and you want to head it off, sit next to them. If you

Figure 11.1   One-on-one meeting arrangements

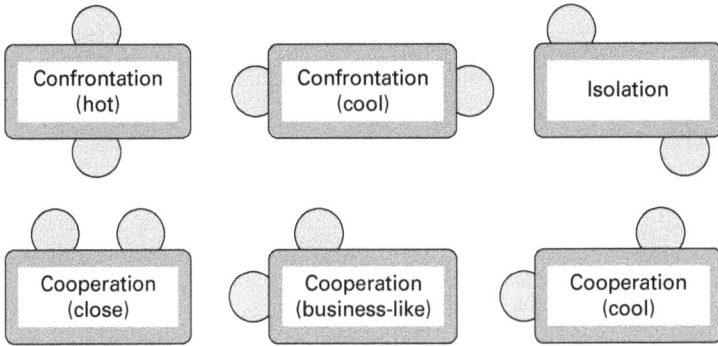

need to, pick up a chair and move it there. Not too so close that it will feel like an aggressive or disrespectful move, but close enough that you are clearly side-by-side. This way there will be no direct face-to-face contact, and they will have to lower their voice if they don't want to escalate deliberately.

A good mid-point between alignment and opposition is to sit at right angles to each other. This is often a good default option.

This brings us to distance. The closer you are, the more intimate you will feel. The further away you are, the more this represents psychological distance between you. A firm rule is to respect their social bubble. We all have one. It is the distance a person can approach before we feel uncomfortable with the proximity. Where their bubble is depends on:

- Cultural norms – some cultures tolerate greater physical closeness.

- Context – in one culture, different contexts allow different degrees of closeness. Just ask anyone on the London Underground!

- Relationship – the better you know one another and the more intimate your relationship, the smaller your bubble with that person becomes. In the workplace, if in doubt, assume a big bubble.

- The person – we each have our own personal preferences. Some people like closeness, while others find it uncomfortable.

In a negotiating room, you can control the level of emotional closeness with the spacing of your seats. Distance takes the heat out of confrontation and the intimacy out of collaboration.

Team negotiation

We have also been considering negotiations with teams of negotiators. This makes the room placement psychology a whole lot more complex. There are no hard-and-fast rules, not least because it would be hard to account for the infinite variety of possibilities. But there are some principles that we can often observe at play.

To do this, we are going to fill our meeting room, one player at a time. We'll start with the power position, and this will be where the primary negotiator (P) sits. They can determine the best position from a combination of geometry and view.

Geometry will place the prime position at the end of a long table. If there is no end seat, the next best is a central position. But, on a round table, there is no end nor central position. This makes round tables ideal for non-adversarial negotiations. If you can arrange for one of these, you can create a small nudge towards a more collaborative mindset.

In terms of the position in the room, the view, the best place to sit is facing the door. Having your back to the door can often appear weak and is certainly a little less comfortable. However, there are other factors to consider when choosing a position based on the view. First, where is the action? If there are going to be presentations, then facing the presenter with the best view is ideal. An alternative is to be closest to the presenter – particularly if you aim to ally yourself with what the presenter will say or what they represent, politically.

Lesser considerations are the positioning with respect to other participants, the windows or other amenities in the room.

Next come the secondary positions (S), which will ideally be occupied by the main advisors, confidantes or assistants to the

Figure 11.2 Negotiating room positions

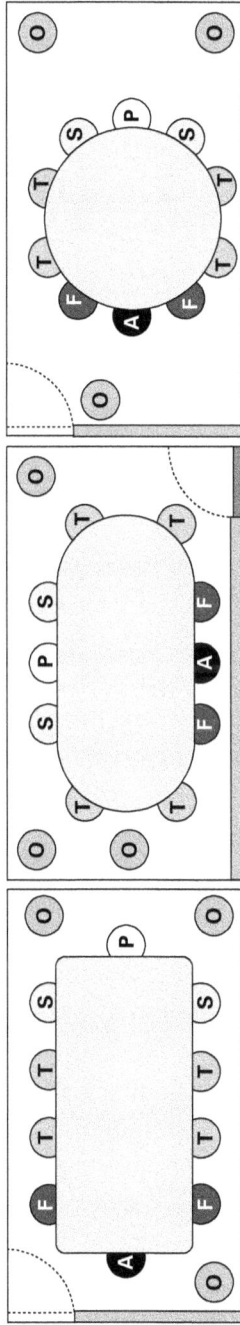

primary negotiator. These people are both allies and people who will want to share some of the reflected glory of the leading player. They will typically choose places next to the primary negotiator or be invited to take them.

The tertiary positions (T) are where the lead negotiator's other supporters are likely to sit. These are positions around the table that have a clear view of the primary player. More important, the lead negotiator will have a clear view of them. Their level of influence is likely to correlate, to a degree, with their proximity and eye contact: the nearer they are, or the stronger the eye contact, the more influence. Inevitably, these two factors can conflict in some room layouts.

Sometimes, there may be an advisor who is more distant, but easy to see. This person might have a subtle influence from their body language, gestures or expressions. This might be someone upon whom the lead negotiator relies for a trusted assessment of something that is going on in the room.

The antagonist position (A) is usually directly opposite the primary negotiator. This is the lead negotiator for the other side, and they will often select a seat that is directly opposite, to give strong, direct eye contact. The full width of their body faces their opposite number. This is also the greatest distance, physically, from the other lead, and therefore metaphorically the greatest distance, and so is the maximally adverse position.

Their followers (F) sit near them – largely mirroring the other team. If there is a power imbalance between the teams, this lower-power team may be fewer in number and may not have the luxury of good eye contact with their leader.

There may be other advisors, supporting participants and observers (O) who will be supporting their team from a greater distance. They might not sit around the main table. If this is the case, they will probably place their seats against the wall. They will only participate in the discussion when called on. Being out of the eye line of the principal negotiators is ideal, because it would be easy for them to do things that may distract, like looking up references or stepping out of the room to access information.

Bias

The last piece of practical psychology is critical, but not because it will help you make an agreement. Rather, because it can help you avoid a bad agreement. This is because human beings are wired to take shortcuts in our thinking. This means we often leap to a conclusion that may not find solid support in the evidence. And, having leapt to the wrong answer, our dislike of being seen to change our mind, and showing we may have made a mistake, can lock that bad judgment into a bad agreement, a bad contract and a bad outcome.

Psychologists call these shortcuts 'heuristics'. A lot of the original research into this was conducted by Daniel Kahneman and Amos Tversky. Kahneman's book, *Thinking, Fast and Slow*, is essential reading for any negotiator or decision-maker. These heuristics are based on the needs of our ancient ancestors to make rapid decisions that would save their lives in an environment filled with mortal dangers.

As bad as office life can feel at times, there is little chance of a lion attacking you from the undergrowth. Yet, these adaptively beneficial thinking patterns are still wired into our 21st-century brains. And they lead to bias. That is, unless we make a conscious effort to override it, our brains will grab onto a conclusion based on weak evidence that may be completely false.

Earlier, we saw the example of loss aversion. We have a bias to resist a loss over seeking a gain. The bias values a marginal gain as having a lesser value than the same degree of loss. This makes the fear of losing something more motivating than the prospect of gaining something equivalent. So, to give something up, we need a concession of greater real value to balance the higher perceived value of what we are losing. We can use this by highlighting the potential losses to the other party if they cannot reach an agreement, rather than focusing solely on gains if they can.

This of course runs us straight into the sunk cost bias. It inclines us to focus on all the time, effort, reputational capital and even money that we have invested so far. It makes it hard for us to back down from a losing position because of what we have put in. But the truth is that the only cost to consider is what we have yet to commit, because that is all we can control. If the benefit we can gain does not exceed what it will cost to get it, we must walk away.

Of many biases, there are three more to highlight as particularly relevant to negotiators.

The first, in order of increasing danger, is *availability bias*. This considers something to be more likely or more frequent if we can more easily bring examples of it to mind. This leaves us prey to recent news items and anecdotal evidence. It is related to the recency, or recall-ability, trap that leads us to give undue weight to recent, dramatic events.

One thing that can distinguish a true professional expert from a skilled non-expert is the *overconfidence bias*. This leads us to over-estimate our abilities, preparation or leverage. It can set us up for mistakes, omissions and unrealistic demands of the other party. This is why you need to check and check again, and seek the advice and objectivity of trusted colleagues.

Without a doubt, the one bias that has the greatest and most damaging effects on society is *confirmation bias*, also called the confirming evidence trap. This makes it far easier for us to notice and incorporate evidence that confirms our prior beliefs or understanding of the situation. When we re-label those beliefs and that understanding with a charged word, which is also correct, we can see the danger. These are prejudices. Confirmation bias not only leads to us favouring supporting evidence, it also leads us to discount evidence that contradicts our beliefs, understanding and prejudices. This is why we need to be open to challenge from contrarian points of view.

Summary points

- You need to be aware and in control of your emotional responses.

- Reactance is our tendency to resist what we perceive as a push, or a restriction on our choices.

- Empathy is a powerful way to see the world from another person's point of view and therefore influence them more effectively.

- There are multiple sources of power in a negotiation.

- Choosing a position around the negotiating table can emphasize or subtly undermine power.

- There are many biases that can cause us to miss important information and evaluate a situation poorly.

12
Teamworking

A team is a small number of people who work together to achieve a shared goal

By number, the vast majority of your negotiations will be simple day-to-day, one-on-one negotiations. They will be short and involve just you and the person you are negotiating with. For many managers and supervisors, these will be the only type of negotiations you conduct. If that's you at the moment, feel free to skip this chapter!

But, for some managers, you will find yourself involved in larger, longer negotiations that involve a team of people on each side. Typical roles where you may get involved in these types of negotiation include:

- senior management roles
- project, programme, portfolio or transformation leadership roles
- procurement and contract negotiation roles
- supply and logistics roles
- sales roles

There are many team roles that you may need. This chapter has a section each for 15 roles, which may sound daunting. In reality, you won't need all of them but you may want to use this as a checklist. It's also important to note that you will often see one individual playing two, three or more of these roles. You could cover the whole roster of roles with a three- or four-person team.

In fact, let's go further. It rarely helps to make your team too large. This can leave some people feeling like a spare part, and others feeling free to shun their responsibilities. Make sure you've covered all the roles you really need with people who can perform them well. Be rigorous in selecting (and excluding) people to forge a team that can work together well and negotiate effectively.

Working together

If you have the right team or, let's face it, the best team you can get, you must pay attention to some team orientation before you go into the negotiation. During the preparation step, make time to ensure you are all briefed and ready to act together as one team:

- Build a good working relationship with each person. Find out a bit about each one, and discuss with them how best they feel you can deploy their experience and capabilities.

- Get the team working together – preparing and planning is an excellent team-building activity that allows each person to appreciate the expertise of their colleagues.

- Discuss with each team member their responsibilities. It can help to draw up a responsibility matrix (there is a template in Appendix 5). This will help you confirm all the critical roles are filled and there are no unplanned overlaps. Then, you can use it to communicate the role allocations to the team, so you all have a shared understanding.

- Draw up a teamworking plan. This sets some ground rules about how you will collaborate inside and outside the formal negotiations. Once again, the best way to do this is as a team discussion. It is a good opportunity for the allocated note taker to practise their craft.

- Ensure that everybody knows how to signal to the lead negotiator that they believe it's necessary to take time out. This will usually be when they have a concern, an observation or some information that the leader needs to know before proceeding.

- Discuss your performance expectations with each team member. Use the conversation to listen to their ideas, advice and concerns.

During a long negotiation, use short breaks to allow each team member to share impressions of where you are, express any concerns and make suggestions. Use the power of the team to work on problems like roadblocks or relationship challenges.

In longer breaks you should also do a quick performance review to allow the team to self-assess its performance and suggest lessons learned that it could apply in the next round.

Top tip
More, less, stop, start, stay review

There are many formats a team can use to efficiently review its performance. One that works well looks for five approaches to different aspects of what you have been doing. In this format, you ask the team to discuss, in turn, what it should:

- do more of
- do less of
- stop doing
- start doing
- stay doing as we are

Alternatively, they can write ideas on sticky notes and place them in boxes on a simple chart.

Figure 12.1   More, less, stop, start, stay

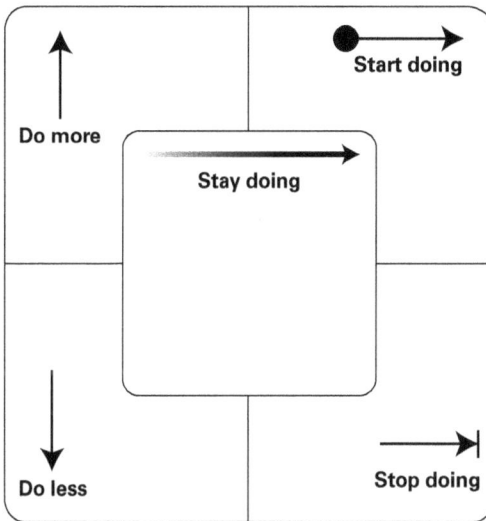

You may also want to have more private conversations with individual team members, to offer your own feedback on, and recognition of, their individual performance. A critical point to remember, however, is to praise in public (in front of the whole team) and to criticize in private (one-to-one). And never criticize a colleague in front of members of the counterparty.

There will be one more chance to review your team's and each individual's performance after the negotiation has finished, following Step 4, Close.

Checklist
Team negotiating roles

Here is a checklist of potential negotiating roles to consider. The rest of the chapter will look at each one:

- Lead negotiator (and deputy lead negotiator)
- Good cop and bad cop (in some cultures this can work, but take care and check your ethical compass)

- Performance coach (for lead negotiator and other team members) and team coach
- Observer
- Analyst (you may also need a specific financial analyst)
- Technical adviser (or subject matter expert)
- Strategy adviser
- Legal adviser (or counsel)
- Cultural adviser
- Risk manager
- Relationship manager
- Note taker (or scribe or rapporteur)
- Administrator (who would usually also take care of logistics)
- Red team (or contrarian or devil's advocate)
- Ultimate decision-maker (if they are not leading the negotiation)

Team negotiating roles

Lead negotiator

The lead negotiator is the person who leads the negotiation. They will present the position and advocate for it persuasively. They are usually responsible for final decision-making and closing the agreement. However, in some cases, they may not. They might only be responsible for leading the negotiation up to the wrap-up of the bargaining stage, before reverting to a decision-maker for a decision. They may then come back, empowered to close. The role of 'decision-maker' is discussed below.

They will, however, make decisions in the room. They will be the one who responds to proposals and selects the requests to make and concessions to offer and agree to. If a team member believes they need to depart from their briefing or agreed plan, they will need the lead negotiator to approve this. If necessary, they will need to send a signal to the lead negotiator requesting a time out to explain their recommendation.

Two other roles related to the lead negotiator role:

1 **A deputy lead negotiator** who will act as a stand-in, should the lead negotiator be indisposed.

2 **A team leader** who is not the lead negotiator. While the lead negotiator focuses outwards, on the negotiation and the counterparty, the team leader focuses on leading and supporting the team. It will be they who facilitates discussions, feedback and problem-solving among the team.

Good cop and bad cop

In some cultures, the practice of two negotiators playing 'good cop' and 'bad cop' can work. But take care and check what is appropriate culturally, and where your ethical compass points are.

The lead negotiator can take one of these roles and another team member the other.

The good cop role will focus on the relationship with the counterparty. They will listen carefully and pick up on subtle messages, showing they see the counterparty's point of view. They will act as a friend. This role is not unlike that of the relationship manager, discussed below, but will be less overtly supportive to the counterparty.

The bad cop role will work to identify and call out potential flaws and problems in the other side's proposals. By becoming a focus for the opposing side's frustration, they allow the lead negotiator to seem fair and supportive by contrast.

Performance coach

Every would-be high performer can benefit from a performance coach. They would certainly support the lead negotiator and may support other team members too.

The coach may or may not attend the negotiation meetings because their role is to provide coaching support outside the negotiation. They help the participants to reflect on how they performed and to identify ways to achieve their goals in the next session.

There may also be a role for a team coach, who would work with the team as a group to bring out the best in collaborative performance. They may act as an intermediary between the lead negotiator and the rest of the team. A team leader could play the role of team coach.

Observer

An important, but often under-valued, role is that of observer. This is someone who will do nothing in the meeting other than observe the dynamics in the room, to look out for the subtle language and nonverbal signals, to pay attention to the details of proposals that are made and to be thinking about them.

They provide feedback to:

- the lead negotiator, about things they may have missed whilst focusing on their own negotiating role;
- individual team members, about their contributions;
- the team as a whole, about the team performance and how they might improve.

Analyst

The analyst is highly adept at analysing the implications of any proposal in real time. They can assess the value and risks to their team and offer suggestions for beneficial ways forward. They will also evaluate suggestions that come up in team discussions when working on problems or roadblocks. When needed, they will also provide formal reports to the team or to decision-makers and governance bodies within the organization.

The analyst may be focused on, for example, strategic, operational, commercial or financial concerns. The financial analyst role is, perhaps, most common. They evaluate the financial implications of any negotiating terms using sophisticated financial modelling tools, such as scenario analysis and discounted cash flows.

Legal adviser

One very specific form of advice will only be necessary in a limited range of circumstances. But where detailed legal language is part of the negotiation, rather than a documentation of the final agreement, you will need legal counsel in the room. You may also need a legal adviser if there are potential legal or regulatory compliance issues, or if the possible structure of the transaction could offer particular risks or benefits.

Technical adviser or subject matter expert (SME)

You will usually need somebody present who has deep knowledge about the technical aspects of what you are negotiating about. Indeed, for big, complex topics, you may need more than one expert – perhaps a whole team of them! These might include legal or financial experts, which are covered above.

The SME role is to support the team with technical advice, provide credibility for the team and assess the implications, opportunities and risks of any negotiating tactic.

Strategy adviser

What if the negotiation is bigger or more complex than any of your team has the experience to deal with confidently? In this case, you may want someone to advise the team on negotiating strategy and tactics. This would be an expert negotiator – possibly an external consultant – who can bring a focus on the goals, strategy and tactics that the team will deploy. They will be able to guide the team on the implications of different proposals, counteroffers or concessions they could make, in response to unfolding events. And they will be highly skilled at reading the room. They will also be able to help the team see past short-term gains and see the whole chess game, many moves ahead.

Cultural adviser

This is another role that you won't often see. However, if you are negotiating within an unfamiliar cultural context, this can prevent serious damage to a relationship arising from an unintended slight, discourtesy or offence. The obvious example is a negotiating team from one country, travelling to negotiate with a team from another, very different country.

A cultural adviser can guide the team on etiquette, expectations and use of language. They may also act as a translator. Beyond this, they may also be able to help the team to frame their proposals in ways that are most compelling to the counterparty, and interpret the counterparty's offers and requests where they may seem hard to understand.

Risk manager

Risk management is everyone's responsibility, and the team may already have advisers who can identify and mitigate risks arising from requests and potential concessions. However, in a negotiation with significant consequences or specific potential risks, a dedicated risk manager may be a valuable asset. Their job is to identify and evaluate risks and put in place mitigation and contingency plans. Ultimately, they will advise whether the risk profile is so damaging to the value of a potential agreement that the team should walk away and prefer to accept its BATNA.

Relationship manager

Another highly specialized role is that of relationship manager. Their focus will be on the relationship rather than the content of the negotiation. Early on, they will lead on building trust and rapport and, as the negotiation progresses, they will shift their focus to keeping communication flowing and working to resolve any conflicts or relationship breakdowns. Their role may extend beyond the negotiations cycle, as they transition to a long-term relationship manager.

Note taker

A role that is likely to be needed in any team negotiation is that of note taker. It has many names, but this is the clearest. You may hear the terms recorder, rapporteur or communications lead, for example. Their task is simple to state: to maintain a complete and accurate record of what is said and agreed. It is possible that the parties may mutually agree on a neutral note taker, but it is more common for each to keep their own record. It is also possible that this role doubles with another, like a relationship manager, strategic adviser or administrator. It's a great role for a junior person to take, as it allows them to be in the room and learn by observing. In the last few years, this role has increasingly been filled by artificial intelligence software tools.

Either way, it's important for the negotiating team to have a clear and complete record. Having someone who can take accurate but concise notes and is focused on doing only that can be very valuable.

Administrator

A big team, working over a long period, may need someone to handle admin and logistics for them. Typical examples of where an administrator can help are with:

- arranging meeting places
- providing equipment and refreshments
- coordinating schedules with the other party

- making travel and accommodation arrangements
- keeping the team updated and circulating notes

Red team

A red team is a second team of equally smart and knowledgeable people, who can work independently to find solutions or critically review the solutions that a prime team develops. This is a big investment. However, a negotiating team may contain someone whose role is to scrutinize, critique and challenge every move the team makes, from a contrarian perspective. This role is often called 'devil's advocate' or contrarian.

Negotiating success will be based in large part on the assumptions, arguments and strategies the team adopts. Having someone to review and challenge them is a powerful way to prevent the onset of groupthink. This is where the team comes to accept ideas because nobody wants to express their concerns for fear of either upsetting the team harmony or facing ridicule. But if this is someone's role, they can do so with impunity.

The role can double with others, especially advisers or a risk manager. But it is one any negotiating team should have.

Ultimate decision-maker

Sometimes – and this is often a result of culture – the lead negotiator will not be the ultimate decision-maker. Whilst they may be in the room observing, or acting as strategy adviser behind the scenes, this individual may not be present for the discussions.

However, once the team has reached the wrap-up, they will refer the decision to close, or to agree to a closure proposal, to the ultimate decision-maker. It is they who have the authority to make decisions on critical concessions and finally approve or reject an agreement on behalf of the organization. They will have an overview of organizational policies, financial constraints and strategy.

If your counterparty has an ultimate decision-maker of this kind, you need to know as early in the negotiation as possible. This is why establishing the authority of the other party to negotiate is a key part of the Opening step in the negotiation process.

Summary points

- A big negotiation needs a team, and there are many roles to consider.

- Keep the team as small as you can, but make it as large as it needs to be.

- Ensure that the team prepares well, and everyone knows their roles.

- Have frequent reviews of negotiating progress and team performance.

13
Traps

Your level of attention to detail can be the difference between success and failure

I don't want to suggest that your negotiating partner will set out to trap you. But the fact is that there are plenty of traps that an unwary negotiator can step into. So, the purpose of this chapter is to alert you to those traps, so you can spot them and then either walk around them or stop before stepping into them.

Overlap/no overlap

Trap number 1 is pursuing an agreement that is not there.

Let's look at an example.

EXAMPLE Is a deal possible... or not?

Two powerful business owners are negotiating over the purchase of a business by one from the other. The negotiations are at deadlock and neither party can unlock the process and make progress. The only people benefiting from this are their lawyers. Finally, the penny drops. One of the negotiators says to the other:

I don't know whether we can reach an agreement. So we need to find an arbiter whose integrity we both trust absolutely. I will put the lowest price I will accept for my business into a sealed envelope and pass it to that person. If you are prepared to put the highest price you would pay for my business into another sealed envelope, we can ask this person to tell us just one thing. Assuming we have made our best offers, is there a chance that we can reach an agreement?

They both did so, and the arbiter told them that they were never going to come to an agreement. They stood down their legal teams and saved themselves a lot of wasted time and legal fees.

In this example, the role of the arbiter was to discover whether there was an overlap between the ranges of prices each negotiator was prepared to offer or accept. This overlap is called the zone of possible agreement, or ZOPA. If there is no overlap, then no amount of bargaining will result in an agreement, so there's no reason to negotiate. In everyday negotiation, you'll need to keep negotiating and testing ideas, until you conclude that there is no ZOPA.

A nice way to think about the ZOPA is as two circles. One circle represents all the possible agreements that I might be prepared to accept and the other represents all the possible agreements that you might be prepared to accept. The boundaries of the circles represent each party's BATNA (best alternative to a negotiated agreement). The question is, do these circles overlap? If they do, that overlap represents your zone of possible agreement. This is your scope for negotiating an agreement that will benefit both parties.

However, one of the negotiators might assess the other's BATNA to be somewhere other than where it actually is. So, their perceived scope for negotiation may be smaller or larger than the true scope for negotiation.

Figure 13.1   Zone of possible agreement

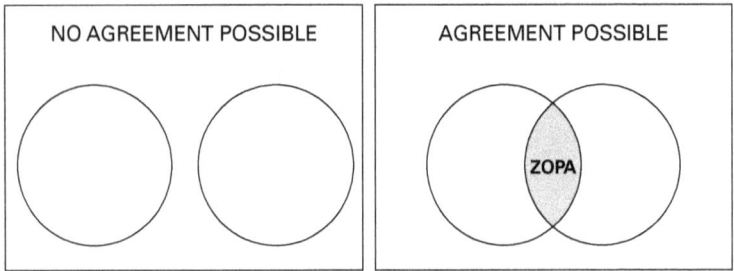

This is important because we base our negotiation strategy on our perceptions of the scope for negotiation; it's all we can do. The other party won't reveal their walk-away point until very late in the process. And neither would you. So, if you sense that the scope for negotiation is small, you will need to trigger some way to test whether there is any scope for agreement, like one of the characters in the case study. You will hope to find out whether there is a ZOPA within which you can make a deal.

Understanding this concept of a scope for agreement, or ZOPA, is essential. It's a simple idea, but without it, you can waste a lot of time.

> The corollary to trap number 1 is the trap of missing the opportunity for a negotiated agreement, by not being aware of the zone of possible agreement.

If you give up on negotiating too early, you may miss out on some form of offer or concession that can create an agreement. This may require deeply creative thinking and broadening the scope of the discussion. So, don't give up on your negotiation until you're sure it cannot succeed, or you may miss making a good deal.

Yes/no

Trap number 2 is making the other party feel like you are manipulating them.

The whole purpose of a negotiation is to get to a place where both parties can say 'yes' to the same thing. 'Yes' is the goal of negotiating. The catch is that, if you try to manoeuvre the other party into saying yes, they can feel like you are trying to manipulate them. At best, they won't feel in control of the conversation. At worst, they will see your tactics as disrespectful or even abusive.

Questions that you have structured to get a 'no', on the other hand, can leave the other party feeling like they are more in control. After all, they are saying 'no' to you! This is more likely to leave them feeling comfortable with you as a negotiator, and can therefore help build rapport.

'Yes' questions can be manipulative. Asking questions that get you to say yes to a first question, and then to a second question, and then to a third question, might get you into a 'yes habit' and perhaps make you likely to say yes to my fourth question.

And that's why 'yes' questions in negotiation have got a bad reputation. Poor negotiators and low-integrity salespeople think that all they have to do is ask questions that get a yes, and they will build a rapport. This way, when they ask for the close, they will get an automatic 'yes'. Even if you think this works (and it rarely will), don't do this.

The corollary to trap number 2 is the trap of not building agreement.

This does not mean that there is no place in negotiation for questions to which the answer is 'yes'. Of course there is! Use them to test and find common ground that you can both agree on. It is the common ground that builds rapport and helps to move you both towards a satisfactory outcome.

Using 'yes' questions properly is an important part of good negotiation. But, if you try to use your 'yes' questions to build a habit of saying yes so that it becomes automatic, then you are being manipulative and you will poison the relationship.

My ultimate advice is simple: don't overthink it. Build yes and no questions into the natural flow of your negotiations and notice the impact they have. Over time, you will get better at calibrating whether to frame a question with the hope of getting a 'yes' answer or of getting a 'no' answer. If you are still at the beginning of your negotiating career, try to understand people by observing reactions and behaviours. Later, you can start to use that understanding to help you ask more carefully crafted questions that can get better results, more quickly.

First/second

Trap number 3 is stating your position too early.

Stating your position early is a trap. Ideally, you will want to wait until the other party has stated their opening position before you state yours. That way, if theirs is less assertive than you had expected, you may want to revise your opening position to try and secure an even better agreement.

The problem with this is that they will be thinking the same thing. They will want you to state your opening position before they state theirs. This could be your first point of conflict, so you will need to weigh up whether this small negotiating advantage is worth the potential for early conflict. So, what are your options?

- If they seem intransigent, you might choose to pragmatically accept that you will put your position on the table first.

- You could make this a first concession and either hope they respect it and reciprocate later, or signal that you are making a concession and will want something in return.

- You could choose to be intransigent and refuse to state your position first.

- You could each put your position in writing and exchange notes.

> The first corollary to trap number 3 is the trap of not stating your position first if it is too far from the other party's position.

If your opening position is too far from theirs, then when you state it after they have stated theirs, you can come across as willingly derailing the negotiation from the start.

A surprising opening position is one that is more extreme than they're expecting. For example, this could be because either:

- as a buyer, you want to strike an agreement for a price that is substantially lower than their standard rate; or

- as a seller, if you're going to be asking for a price that is significantly higher than you think the buyer will be expecting.

In Chapter 11, Psychology, we saw the anchoring effect. When a negotiation starts with an opening position, the rest of the negotiation is usually about how we are going to move in one direction or another from that point. And we call that point the 'anchor'. If the other party opens with their position first, they set the anchor, and you are negotiating to move it a long way from their expectations.

But, if you can set the anchor, it is the other party who immediately feels that they have a lot of work to do. Now the negotiation is anchored to your position.

And, thinking back to the ZOPA that we discussed above, it means that if the other party hears your opening position and thinks there is no way they can get anywhere near that, you can save yourself a lot of time negotiating where an agreement isn't going to be possible. Of course, there is a risk, if your opening position is too far from your BATNA, that you could therefore miss out on getting an agreement. If this is a strategy, it is a bold (and risky) one.

> The second corollary to trap number 3 is the trap of accepting the first offer you receive, uncritically.

Whatever offer the other party makes as their opening position, don't forget that it is just that: a position. And never accept a good first offer without countering to try to make it a little better. This is not just for your benefit. If they feel they got the deal too easily, they will worry that they could have done better and feel a sense of remorse about the agreement they made. Always treat the first offer you get as an anchor. Respond with a well-crafted counteroffer.

Under-preparing

> Trap number 4 is not preparing thoroughly enough.

Chapter 3, Prepare, tells you everything you need to do. If you go into a negotiation underprepared, you have only yourself to blame if you either fail to reach an agreement or if you reach an agreement that you think is sub-optimal. And that will create guilt and frustration.

Do the work of preparing thoroughly, to avoid handing your counterparty an unearned advantage.

> The corollary to trap number 4 is the trap of assuming your assessment of the other party's interests and priorities is correct, and failing to spot the signs that you need to shift your strategy.

Be aware, however, that no matter how well you prepare, your assessments about the other party can only ever be preliminary – and contingent upon the evidence of their decisions and actions in the negotiation. Asking good questions, listening and observing attentively, and considering everything you learn is the only way to keep an upper hand.

Over-conceding

Trap number 5 is making concessions that are too big.

Let's start with the obvious fact of negotiation. Never make a significant concession unless you can secure an equivalent concession or benefit in return.

The exception to this, of course, is the loss leader principle, where the value you get in return is the relationship itself. But even here, take care to avoid the risk of being seen as a pushover, which can set you up in a subordinate role in the relationship. The strongest relationships are ones of equal partners.

So, always negotiate something of broadly equal value in return for any concession you make.

The next thing to consider is setting yourself up for a runaway series of concessions that can destroy all value. The way to control this starts with knowing your BATNA and having a sensible margin above that to negotiate towards. Your first concession must never exceed half of the distance between your starting position and your target position.

Your next concession should once again be no more than half the remaining distance. And so on… This ensures that your concessions converge on the right end point.

And never immediately give in to an ultimatum; neither should you immediately walk away from the negotiation. Take it as a negotiating stance. Ask questions, listen patiently and explore what

Figure 13.2   Converging concessions

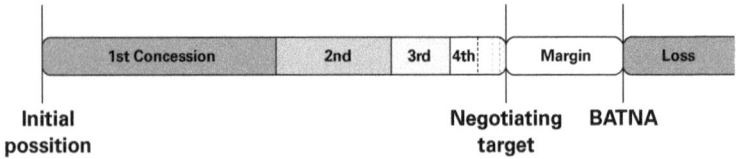

is behind it. Continuing the conversation will help you and your counterpart return to effective give and take of requests, offers and concessions.

> The corollary to trap number 5 is the trap of focusing only on a single factor – usually price – and not seeing the negotiation from all angles. This can lead to missing an opportunity for concessions that create a beneficial agreement.

If you place too much emphasis on one factor, whether it is price, quality, schedule, risk, convenience or anything else, it will unbalance your negotiation and diminish your chance of a mutually satisfying agreement. Always pay attention to the total value of the agreement, including intangible benefits and long-term potential.

Underestimating

> Trap number 6 is underestimating the skills and experience of the other party.

Underestimating the skills and experience of the other party can easily lead to overconfidence and complacency. It is best to research their experience, skills and resources carefully, and to prepare to deal with them properly. But if you cannot find out anything about them, prepare to negotiate with a wily, skilful negotiator who has prepared thoroughly.

And never allow yourself to become cocky and arrogant. That kind of pride does indeed come before a negotiating fall. Stay grounded in the need to pay attention to everything that happens, and do not hesitate to call for a time-out if there is something going on that you cannot figure out.

> The corollary to trap number 6 is the trap of underestimating your own preparation, experience and skills.

Arrogance is bad, but a lack of confidence in yourself and your team is no better. If your counterparty senses any doubt in your own competence, it will be open to them to exploit it. This is yet one more case where balance is everything – this time between confidence and humility.

Overcommitting

> Trap number 7 is overcommitting to a single course of action.

When we talked about bias in Chapter 11, Psychology, we included the sunk cost fallacy. This is an over-focus on what you have already spent, in terms of time, money and reputational commitment. This can lead us to continue to pursue something even when it should be clear that it is no longer the right path.

You need to stay alert to emerging problems with the plan you have, and how the outcome they can lead to is not what you had anticipated. The ability to be flexible and adapt to circumstances is a vital negotiating skill.

If you don't have this, it can lead you to close and accept an outcome that is not good enough. If you become too fixated in following an outdated approach, it can even lead you to an outcome that is poorer than your BATNA, your best alternative to the negotiated agreement.

> The corollary to trap number 7 is the trap of flexing too much and losing sight of your end goal or your BATNA.

Be ready to change your tactics, your plan and even your strategy as soon as the evidence suggests it is no longer optimal. But never lose sight of your BATNA and your goal. Your BATNA is there to act as your ultimate safety net. Your goal is the North Star that will guide you.

Under-relating

> Trap number 8 is focusing too much on the process and tasks at hand, forgetting the importance of the relationship.

Here is another case of balance, but you don't need anyone to hammer that home again. What may be valuable is a reminder of the small traps we fall into that can cumulatively erode the quality of a relationship:

- **Trap 8a is focusing on transactions over relationships**
  Rarely is a negotiation a one-time event. In the workplace, most negotiations will be part of a long-term partnership. And within a negotiation, while each request or offer may seem like a transaction, it sits within the context of an evolving relationship.

  Treating part of the negotiation solely as a transaction can damage trust and reduce the chances of successful future collaborations, either within the negotiation or the wider relationship. So, focus on maintaining a positive relationship and building goodwill for future deals.

- **Trap 8b is neglecting, or failing to be sensitive to, cultural norms**
  A truly inadvertent, minor case of disrespect may have no long-term impact if you are able to spot it and apologize. But if you can tune into and respect the culture in which you are working and the etiquette, communication styles or decision-making process of the other party, you will be less likely to offend or alienate them. So, once again, do your research and adapt your style accordingly.

- **Trap 8c is talking too much and not listening enough**
  Don't be too keen to put your point of view. Prioritize curiosity and employ questioning, listening and silence as your main communication modes. The more you say, particularly if it comes across as defending your position, the less you'll learn and the weaker you will look. In a team negotiation, ask one of the team to keep track of your speaking, silence and listening times.

- **Trap 8d is not paying attention to non-verbal cues**
  Non-verbal cues include body language like posture, movement, gesture and expression, along with vocal patterns like tone of voice, pace, volume and inflection. Even if you don't know the 'rules' for interpreting them, by observing carefully, you will pick up hints of wariness, enthusiasm, frustration or anger, for example. And the more you do this, the better you'll get at it. Use the information you acquire to tweak your style and maybe your requests and offers.

- **Trap 8e is allowing your emotions to show**
  If you show anger, frustration or joy, without intending to, you are giving away negotiators' gold! And if you let those emotions drive you to be careless, aggressive or confrontational you'll compromise trust and damage any collaborative spirit. You could even sink the negotiation.

The corollary to trap number 8 is the trap of trying too hard.

Important as it is to focus on the relationship, please do not try too hard and risk losing your sense of professionalism in an attempt to 'be their friend'. Respect may draw you to a negotiating partner who may become a professional friend. But that is not the goal of negotiation. At best it can harm your objectivity; at worst it can undermine your credibility as a negotiator.

Overcomplicating

Trap number 9 is overcomplicating a simple negotiation.

This book has a lot of ideas in it. But remember, some negotiations are short and simple. Treat them that way. Don't try to be too clever by introducing too many techniques or overloading the discussion with details. This can cause confusion, undermine your credibility and slow down the whole process. Ask yourself what the essence of the negotiation is, and what are the minimum set of things you need to do, focus on and track.

The corollary to trap number 9 is the trap of not following the process; in particular, forgetting some of the important elements of following up.

However, details matter and if you miss something important, particularly in following up, you can undermine the whole process. Be rigorous in planning and executing on your follow-up responsibilities.

Losing control

Trap number 10 is losing self-control.

Emotional self-control is one of the few master skills for professionals in any field, and its importance in negotiating should be
self-evident. If you feel yourself getting triggered by something and
becoming aggressive or accusatory, it's time to ask for a time-out.
Take a deep breath, ask for a break or simply excuse yourself for a
few minutes. Aggression, rudeness or any form of disrespect can
derail a negotiation and damage a relationship for the long term.

Even at a lower level, try not to allow stress and anxiety to
impact your words, tone or demeanour. Pressure is a part of negotiation and it's natural to feel it. And it can result in nervousness,
fidgeting and a lack of confidence. So, reframe your anxiety as
excitement and the pressure as importance. Those butterflies in
your stomach mean you are ready!

Another problem with losing emotional self-control is the risk
of saying or doing something on impulse, without consideration.
This can lead unskilled negotiators to flare up, throw insults or
pack up and walk out of the room.

If you do become frustrated or worse, and say something you
should not have said or handle yourself in a way that is less than
wholly professional, take action to correct it immediately.
Homespun wisdom gives us the perfect formula:

- 'fess-up
- say you are sorry
- make it right, if you can
- move on

> The corollary to trap number 10 is the trap of not knowing when to walk away or, worse, not having the courage to.

Sometimes, you do need to recognize that the negotiation itself has got out of control. This means that, if you cannot restore control, you need the courage to walk away. Staying with a negotiation when the terms are clearly unfavourable, or behaviours have deteriorated, is a mistake. You could end up agreeing to terms that are not in your interests. The walk away may be temporary or permanent, but don't let yourself get sucked into a downward spiral.

Summary points

- Trap number 1 is pursuing an agreement that is not there.
  - The corollary to trap number 1 is the trap of missing the opportunity for a negotiated agreement by not being aware of the zone of possible agreement.
- Trap number 2 is making the other party feel like you are manipulating them.
  - The corollary to trap number 2 is the trap of not building agreement.
- Trap number 3 is stating your position too early.
  - The first corollary to trap number 3 is the trap of not stating your position first if it is too far from the other party's position.
  - The second corollary to trap number 3 is the trap of accepting the first offer you receive uncritically.
- Trap number 4 is not preparing thoroughly enough.
  - The corollary to trap number 4 is the trap of assuming your assessment of the other party's interests and priorities is correct and failing to spot the signs that you need to shift your strategy.

- Trap number 5 is making concessions that are too big.

    o The corollary to trap number 5 is the trap of focusing only on a single factor – usually price – and not seeing the negotiation from all angles. This can lead to missing an opportunity for concessions that create a beneficial agreement.

- Trap number 6 is underestimating the skills and experience of the other party.

    o The corollary to trap number 6 is the trap of underestimating your own preparation, experience and skills.

- Trap number 7 is overcommitting to a single course of action.

    o The corollary to trap number 7 is the trap of flexing too much and losing sight of your end goal or your BATNA.

- Trap number 8 is focusing too much on the process and tasks at hand, forgetting the importance of the relationship.

    o The corollary to trap number 8 is the trap of trying too hard.

- Trap number 9 is overcomplicating a simple negotiation.

    o The corollary to trap number 9 is the trap of not following the process; in particular, forgetting some of the important elements of following up.

- Trap number 10 is losing self-control.

    o The corollary to trap number 10 is the trap of not knowing when to walk away or, worse, not having the courage to.

14
Problems
Shift happens!

The path of negotiation will not always be straight and smooth. There will be bends, forks, bumps and obstacles in your way. You've seen some of them already, earlier in the book. In this chapter, we'll focus on an escalation from bad behaviour to getting stuck and then deadlock. We'll end with an introduction to resolving conflict and what to do if a relationship breaks down.

For all of these, however, there is one simple rule. Keep your cool. High levels of emotion will never help and can lead to a worsening of the situation. Take a break if you feel yourself getting frustrated, upset or angry. Use a time-out to calm yourself, examine what is making you feel the way you do and plan a next step to get the negotiation back on track.

Bad behaviour

The first problem you might encounter is bad behaviour. But what is 'bad behaviour'? The answer must lie in the eye of the beholder, and it is important to know that what you consider to be my 'bad behaviour' may, for me, just be my attempt to do my best, get what I think I deserve and be heard. This means that you might deprecate the way I express myself – the behaviour – but you must always respect me, the person.

Usually, bad behaviour is behaviour that is inappropriate for the context. The early signs that something's going wrong are not usually hard to spot if you stay alert for them. They will easily escalate if no one does anything active to counter the trend:

- someone is not paying attention or listening to what others are saying
- increased levels of tension in the room
- defensive responses to your assertions
- signs of withdrawal and perhaps sulky behaviour
- low-level personal attacks, like sarcasm, snarky comments and put-downs
- direct attacks on someone's personality or even their integrity

You know someone is starting to lose control when they raise their voice, not to be heard, but to dominate the conversation. These signs of negotiation going bad mean you need to find ways to deal with it.

Wisdom from *Getting to Yes*

In their book, *Getting to Yes*, Roger Fisher and William Ury recommend you 'separate the people from the problem'. Whether you like someone or not, you need to respect them and deal with the problem. If you can, make them your ally. Fisher and Ury recommend three things that will help:

1 Try to understand how they perceive the world, by putting yourself in their shoes. Look at the problem from their point of view to understand what matters to them. In this case, what is causing their behaviour?

2 Recognize and understand the emotions in the room without reacting to them and becoming emotional yourself. If you need to let off steam, call a time-out and do it outside the negotiating room.

3 Good communication is how we can build understanding. Speak openly and honestly about what you see, hear and understand about the situation. Don't put words into their mouth by telling them what they should think or feel, but listen to them without interrupting or challenging them.

There are some forms of bad behaviour that crop up a lot in negotiations. Let's recognize some of them and see what you can do to counter them appropriately.

Aggressive behaviour

Let's start with simple aggressive behaviour, which could either be inadvertent or an attempt to intimidate you. This can lead in several directions but they all start with you feeling disrespected. But you need to be careful. If all you do is say something like, 'There's no point in getting angry' then you're more likely to fuel the anger than to subdue it.

Instead, allow them to express their emotions and then start to label them: 'It sounds to me like you're very angry.' Next, invite them to explain what is making them angry. As we move from expressing our emotions to explaining them, we move our mental focus from the parts of our brain that deal with emotions to the parts that deal with logic and reason. And that will start to diffuse the emotional intensity.

As you listen to the other person's point of view, repeat back their concerns, opinions and priorities to them, so they know you're understanding them. Listen carefully for clues to the issues that lie beneath anger. Then, as their temper cools, discuss those issues and the differences between their position and yours. Now, with a calmer demeanour, they will be ready to negotiate rationally. Try dividing up the pie to reduce the scope of disagreement.

Power play

Aggression can escalate into a power play, where someone tries to coerce you into a position that you know is wrong for you. This is a form of bullying, so you need to call it out and stand firm. Do this by saying something like, 'It feels to me like you're trying to coerce me into something that I am not ready to do.' Then assert the real choices that you have. Take a time-out if you need to, but state clearly what you want and that you consider it reasonable.

Coercion may hide itself behind outwardly cooperative behaviour. This is deceitful and we call it manipulation. By its nature, it can be hard to spot. It uses tricks and psychological pressure to move you in a direction you wouldn't choose. Deal with it as soon as you detect it, using a technique called fogging.

Fogging is when you neither agree nor disagree with an assertion that they make. Acknowledge their assertion without addressing it. For example, label their assertion like this: 'You think I'm being foolish.' But neither agree nor disagree, because this is a trap. If you accept their point, you are giving in to the manipulation. If you contest it, they can cast you as initiating conflict.

You can also repeat their assertion as a question: 'You think I'm being foolish?' Now they need to either deny it or own it. You win either way, by either clearing the charge or getting their aggression into the open. If they equivocate, for example saying, 'That's not what I said', then take control of the conversation without escalating it into conflict.

The final version of fogging is to simply ignore the manipulative comment and change the subject. Whatever approach you choose, the best way to deal with this kind of passive-aggressive behaviour is to cast a veil of fog over your manipulator.

Ad hominem attack

The example above takes us close to an ad hominem attack. This is a verbal put-down that attacks the person, rather than their actions, words or ideas. They can focus on ability, character or personality, and are a nasty way for someone to go. You could just ignore them, but it's unlikely they will stop at one attack. Instead, recognize that this is another form of bullying and call them out. Calmly say something like, 'This is not appropriate. It feels disrespectful, so please stop.'

Stand your ground without losing your temper or reciprocating. Show them that you are more temperate, more confident and classier than they are!

But what if the attacks continue? Now it's time to ask for an adjournment and, if that doesn't work, consider walking away. But if you are representing your organization, that may not be possible. Instead, consider looking for someone else who can step in. Ideally, this would be someone several steps senior. One step up feels like you just giving in and asking your boss to do it. Several steps senior says you have the support of the organization. It will not put up with that behaviour.

Refusal to move

The last two examples of bad behaviour are opposites of one another. The first is a refusal to shift from a position. This is effectively saying, 'I'm not going to negotiate any further.' This is not a best and final offer (BAFO) or them arriving at their BATNA. This is stubbornness as a deliberate tactic to coerce you into more concessions.

If they have reached their BATNA, they will say something like, 'This is my best and final offer and I cannot move any further. If you can't accept this, I am prepared to walk away.' A stubborn refusal to shift sounds more like, 'This is as far as I want to go, so you need to meet me.'

As before, label the behaviour and say something like, 'This does not sound like a negotiation.' Ask, 'Have you reached your best and final offer? Is this the point at which you're prepared to walk away if we can't agree?' This will flush out what is going on.

If you're convinced that it is stubbornness, then you need to be prepared to call it out and walk away. This makes it their turn; they need to make a move. And, if they're unwilling to, then suggest an adjournment.

Quick fix

The opposite form of bad behaviour might sound like a good result. It's the quick fix. This is a refusal to engage with a problem, so making a quick concession and moving on. It's another refusal to negotiate. At best, it could lead to remorse down the line. At worst, it could threaten your agreement with accusations of coercion.

So, it can be better to have the tough conversation – even an argument – than take the quick win. Say something like, 'It feels like we're not discussing something we need to discuss. Please share your concerns; I would like to hear them.' If they won't do that, you can call for an adjournment: 'It feels like there is something we're not discussing so I suggest an adjournment so we can each consider what the issues might be and how best to address them when we're back in the room.' An alternative is to suggest that each party writes down their concerns. Putting things into writing takes some of the emotion out of the process.

Getting stuck

Sometimes the problem is just what negotiation is all about. It's nobody's fault, but you can't agree… yet. So, take a deep breath and prepare for some work. Maybe even call for a short break and get yourselves fuelled up with a drink and a snack!

It can help to return to the common ground that both parties share. Remind each other how far you've got, to give you both confidence in the progress and goodwill you've achieved. This will fortify you for the next stages of the negotiation.

The most important technique is a combination of exploration and curiosity. Ask each other questions and listen to each other's answers. Return the conversation to interests, priorities and needs, rather than the positions you have each taken. These define the problem, and the solution will be in the overlap. If you can uncover new interests or new ways to think about them, it's usually the new information and new perspectives that lead to a breakthrough.

Top tip
Creativity techniques for finding options

In *Getting to Yes*, Fisher and Ury advocate the need to 'invent options for mutual benefit'. But how can you do that?

To find new ideas, ask the question 'For what purpose?' about each other's interests, priorities and needs. And keep asking the question until the answer is self-evidently true. This will create a higher level of understanding about each other's interests.

Next, ask questions like 'How else can we meet that purpose?' The answers to this question will create new options.

My final tip, if you feel really stuck, is to move to a new venue. Moving yourselves can give you a literally new perspective on things. So, call for a time-out and reconvene somewhere else – even if it is just the next meeting room along.

Deadlock

It's one thing to get stuck, but quite another to feel that there is no route to getting unstuck. This is deadlock. There is no possibility of further progress. The obvious solution is for both parties to walk away, to avoid wasting more time and energy.

However, before you leave the field, is there a way to change the game enough to create the possibility of movement?

You can try the creative approach and apply the 'For what purpose?' question to the problem, asking either:

- 'For what purpose have we got stuck?' or
- 'For what purpose are we trying to resolve this deadlock?'

Follow this up with:

- 'How else can we do what got us stuck?' If you understand what could make the problem worse, you may figure out what the opposite is – and that may make things better.

- 'How else can we serve the reason for getting deadlocked... without being in deadlock?' Deadlock may arise because you both need to save face, look assertive, avoid concessions or any number of reasons. Is there a way to deliver that and move out of deadlock?

A complementary approach is to take a break. Sometimes you need thinking time and some perspective to see a way through. If you can't change the game and you aren't ready to walk off the field, then maybe sitting by the sidelines for a while will help. Give yourselves time to reflect, take advice and think.

If, and only if, you are convinced that you are at deadlock, and there's nothing else to try, then you are left with the last resort: to walk away. But you need to be sure this is the right move, because it may be irrevocable.

Plan how you will do it and what you're going to say. Prepare a simple statement that puts the facts clearly and states your position in a way that is respectful of the other party. Tell them this is your decision and, ideally, do it face to face. Be courteous, polite and respectful, but also firm.

Do not blame the other party. Instead, take your shared responsibility for the breakdown in negotiations and express regret for it. This way, you protect the relationship and leave the door open to come back to the negotiating table later. Be clear that this is a settled decision unless circumstances change.

'Unless circumstances change' is how you can leave the door open to resume negotiations if they can change their position. If they are prepared to move, or if something else happens, let them know you're willing – even keen – to come back to the table.

Then go. Don't hesitate. Don't look back. Pack up your things calmly and quietly, shake hands and leave.

If you do this well then, if circumstances change, you can come back together. But they probably won't. So, that's it: the negotiation has finished.

Deadlock is unfortunate. It isn't what anyone wants from a negotiation. But it does happen. If you have conducted yourself professionally through the negotiation and walking away, the relationship will still be sound. Next time round, you will have a head start and circumstances may be more favourable to a negotiated agreement.

Conflict

If negotiation is conflict conducted respectfully and mediated by a clear process, then if either respect or process break down, all you are left with is conflict. So, what are the ways to de-escalate that conflict?

The first thing you need to do is make the decision to engage positively to resolve the conflict. Having made that decision, reach out to the other person and invite them to do the same. If they do, show them that you appreciate their courage and commitment.

The first skill in conflict management is observation. William James told us that:

> The most important need of the human soul is to be understood.

So, your listening skills and ability to observe are critical to hear what the other person says and to pick up the unspoken messages that betray their growing unease. The more you can understand their point of view and communicate your own, the better. But, as Stephen Covey tells us in the fifth of his *7 Habits of Highly Effective People*:

> Seek first to understand, then to be understood.

Share facts, feelings, perspectives, concerns and definitions to build rapport and understanding. When you have understood one another and the source of the conflict, you need to work together to find criteria for a satisfactory resolution. This means getting past the conflict that is blocking progress in your negotiation – not finishing that negotiation. This will come after you have defused the conflict.

Now you need to explore options for what you can each do to climb down from the conflict. When you have found something that you think will work, offer to take the steps you have agreed on.

Like negotiation, attitude is everything. Be calm, flexible, generous and respectful. And always act in good faith.

Breakdown

If you cannot resolve a conflict, you could see a breakdown in your relationship. Now you will need to repair that breakdown before you can proceed with your negotiation. Here is a 10-step relationship repair process.

1 Declare that a breakdown has occurred
You need to state that there's been a breakdown and what you perceive it to be:

'Last time we spoke, things went wrong, and I feel that our relationship has been damaged.'

Getting this right is the first step in rebuilding trust, so talk about why it matters to you. If you did something wrong, say so and apologize. Don't ask for, or expect, their forgiveness or approval – that's not what this process is for.

2 State the outcomes you want to work towards
Set out the goal you want to achieve. Usually it will be around regaining trust and rebuilding the relationship, so you can continue to negotiate effectively:

'What I would like to achieve is…'

3 Invite them to state their outcomes

Ask them what they want to work towards. They may be content to let the breakdown stand, but this is unlikely. Mending the relationship will be based on the overlap between your and their desired outcomes:

'What would you like us to achieve?'

What if they say, 'I really don't trust you and I don't want to have anything more to do with you'? You have to respect that. You won't win back their respect and their trust by arguing with them.

However, if they do want to rebuild the relationship, it's time to move to step four of the breakdown routine.

4 Share the facts

Be honest about what happened, your own shortcomings and your emotions. Give examples to illustrate this and avoid blaming anyone. Be prepared to acknowledge different interpretations that you and they have of events, and how you each contributed to the problem. Take care to distinguish facts from opinions and share how you feel about the situation:

'What happened last time we met was...'

Invite them to share their perceptions of what happened. When you have a shared understanding of how each of you feels, and how you interpreted the situation, it's time to share your commitments.

5 State your commitments

You might want to reiterate what you have been committed to in the past, but you must focus on what you are committed to now, to help achieve your outcome:

'Having listened to what you have to say, I am committed to...'

6 Invite their commitments

They may decline to make any commitments at this stage because they are not ready to reconcile. But if you want overlapping outcomes, and you have got this far, there is probably some rapport. They will probably feel ready to offer some commitments of their own in return for yours:

'What are you committed to, now?'

7 Look for what is missing

Now you've made your commitments, work together to find out what's missing or broken in the relationship and how to fix it. It may be missing information, poor behaviours or a process that's not working, for example:

'What was missing for me was...'

8 Look for options

Based on what's missing, what do you both need to do to fill the gaps, make things right and mend the breakdown? If you agree you won't be able to mend the breakdown, what are your alternatives? Is there a way to deal with things you both need to contribute to without a good relationship? If so, how?

'Here are some possible ways forward for us... What other ways can you suggest?'

9 Work together to craft a plan

What are the actions, requests, promises, resources and timing you will each commit to, to mend the relationship?

'This is what I propose to do... and this is what I would like from you.'

10 Reiterate your commitment

Once you have a plan, explicitly restate what you are committed to doing, and then invite them to do likewise:

'I think this plan is a good one and I am committed to pursuing it as best I can.'

If the process has worked, they will probably say something similar, in their own way.

Summary points

- There are many forms of bad behaviour, including aggression, coercion, manipulation, ad hominem attacks, stubborn refusal to negotiate and ducking the tough conversation.

- If you get stuck, look for creative options to progress the negotiation.

- If you are deadlocked, you must either change the game, take a time out or walk away.

- Conflict is always a possibility. The most important thing is to build a resolution based on understanding one another and what the source of the conflict is.

- If your relationship breaks down, follow the 10-step relationship repair process to try to restore it.

Part 3
Review

15

Review

Reflection is the path to wisdom

The best way to get better at anything is to do it, to review your experience and then to do it again, incorporating what you have learned the previous times you did it. This of course applies to negotiation, which is a skill that we can develop through practice and reflection.

In this chapter, we will look at three things:

1 How to conduct a team review, so that each team member can learn from their experience.

2 A reflective learning process that you can use, as an individual, whether you had a team to support you or conducted a one-to-one negotiation.

3 A review of the most important messages of this book.

Learning lessons: team negotiations

If you have led a negotiating team, you will have a number of responsibilities to them, even after the negotiation is over – whether or not you have achieved an agreement.

First, of course, if you have been successful, you need to celebrate your team's success in an appropriate way. And, because your negotiation was a success, you may well decide to host a celebration that includes your counterparty and their team. Be careful, whether you celebrate as one team or two, not to crow over a 'victory'. This is not the attitude of a high-integrity negotiator.

A second responsibility to your team is to meet with team members to give them good-quality feedback on their performance. This is a chance to help them start to learn lessons from their individual contributions. If they performed well, focus on recognizing this fact and giving positive feedback. Help them to see what they did well, and how it contributed to the team's success. And prompt them to figure out how they can enhance what they did and make it a professional habit in the future.

For a team member whose performance was below the standard that you expect of them, help them to understand what an appropriate standard will be next time they play a similar role, and what steps they can take to develop their skills to meet that standard. Good feedback is not about blame, but about raising awareness and stimulating a sense of responsibility for performance.

Your third responsibility is to set up and maybe lead a team review of the negotiation, as a chance to reflect on team performance and lessons the team can learn for future performance. In some contexts, this is called a 'retrospective'.

If you are going to lead the retrospective, prepare carefully – just as you did (I hope) for the negotiation itself! Think about a comfortable setting to hold the meeting in and the materials you will need to help facilitate the process. This will be different if it is in person or online. Then plan a structured session that will allow people to discuss what happened during the negotiation and what the team can learn from those events. Set out an agenda and invite everyone in your team to attend.

Start the meeting informally and, as you start the formal part of the meeting, establish the context and ground rules. Remind your colleagues that the purpose is about learning, and that you expect constructive and respectful discussion, not blame, recriminations or personal attacks. People need to feel safe if they are to share mistakes and failings openly. And that means you must role-model good behaviour and actively maintain a safe environment.

As you conduct the conversation, make sure everyone – particularly the shyer members of the team – contributes. Approaches like round-robins (where you call on everyone, one at a time) and silent writing make it easier for a reserved person to contribute.

You can be as structured or as free-form as you like in discussing the negotiation. This will depend on your style, the culture of the team and the scale of the negotiation. If you want to structure your discussion, there is a structured framework for a lessons-learned review in Appendix 6.

At the end of the meeting, summarize the key insights that the team has noted. Better still, task the team, maybe in small groups, to do this. From these key insights, ask the team to prepare an action list of things that will help prepare for, and conduct, a better negotiation next time.

The value of a retrospective is *not* in having a smart Lessons-Learned Document (with capitals!) Rather, it is in the experience the team has in reflecting on their own learning. However, some teams like to have a document to refer to later and some organizations like to have a record. If either of these is true, seek volunteers to prepare a final document.

Finally, close your meeting by:

- offering a personal reflection on what you have learned at the meeting;
- giving appreciation for the work the team has done, both in the negotiation and in the retrospective;
- encouraging everyone to continue their learning and personal professional development;
- thanking people for their attendance and contributions.

And, of course, after your retrospective meeting, do whatever follow-up you need to do, to both meet commitments you made and serve the team that you have led.

Reflective learning: personal development

Whether you have a team or not, you can learn from your experiences by taking time to reflect on them. Indeed, you will benefit enormously if you can make reflection a regular practice, either weekly or even daily. Why not get yourself a nice notebook, to record your insights from this process? Surprisingly soon, you'll find you have an archive of thoughts that you will treasure.

One thing matters more than anything else. This will only work if you are scrupulously honest with yourself. You may not want to commit your blunders and misjudgements to paper, but you must face up to them in your reflection process. Take a long, cold look at the evidence of your experience. Take responsibility for your errors and pride in your successes.

When you do this, there are a number of questions to turn over in your mind, in a relaxing environment – maybe with your choice of drink! These are not well suited to a systematic process; they are prompts that might stimulate interesting thoughts. Some days one or two will seem relevant and, on other days, it may be different questions that trigger valuable insights. The 20 questions below are framed in the context of reflections about negotiation, but you can apply many of the ideas more generally.

Twenty personal reflection questions for negotiators to consider

1 What was the context for this negotiation?

2 Did I go into the negotiation with appropriate and well-formed objectives?

3 How well did I prepare myself and what did I miss?

4 Did I know my BATNA and did I use that knowledge during the negotiation?

5 How strong was the rapport I was able to build with the other party?

6 What aspects of the opening step went well and what would I do differently in future?

7 How suitable was my negotiating strategy and how effectively did I apply it?

8 What aspects of my preparation were most and least helpful in the negotiation?

9 What unexpected turns did the negotiation take and how quickly did I spot them?

10 What could I have realistically done to anticipate the surprises?

11 How well did I adapt to the way my counterparty negotiated and to any surprises in the negotiation?

12 What challenges arose along the way and how did I handle them?

13 Which one of us initiated the close and how did we do it?

14 How did the final agreement compare to my goal and my BATNA?

15 What is the state of my relationship with the counterparty at the end of the negotiation?

16 What is the most important thing to learn from this experience?

17 What is my biggest regret or disappointment?

18 What did I accomplish?

19 What would I do the same, and what differently, if faced with the same scenario?

20 What next?

Review of *How to Negotiate*

At the end of a 'how to' book, you might expect to see a review of the key lessons. And this one won't disappoint you. But the best way to consolidate your learning is not by reading through a checklist of somebody else's key takeaways – not even someone as grand as the author!

It is far better to carry out your own active review of what you have read and build your own summary. Unlike the author's, this will focus on your context, starting point and priorities. So, before presenting you with my own closing summary, I strongly recommend you do this exercise...

Exercise   Personal review of *How to Negotiate*

Before you read the author's assessment of the most important information in *How to Negotiate*, please think about what has been most important for you. You can follow the framework below or use one of your own.

1 **What have been the most interesting and insightful things you learned from this book?**
   List the ideas and information that have changed the way you think about negotiation and your understanding of the negotiating process.

2 **What did you find most practical and useful to you?**
   List the tools, techniques and approaches that you think will be most helpful to you in the kinds of negotiations you expect to be a part of.

3 **What did you find confusing, curious or worth learning more about?**
   List anything you did not understand on first reading. And add to that list anything that sparked your curiosity. What will you do to investigate these things and take your learning further?

4 **Having read this book, what will you do differently next time you need to negotiate?**
   If you don't change your approach, you are unlikely to change the results you get. So, list things you intend to do next time you negotiate.

If you did the exercise above, you really don't need to read what follows. However, human psychology suggests that, if you did do the exercise, you are far more likely to read this! Maybe it's because you want to see if you got it right. Don't worry, you did. Or perhaps you want to see if the author got it right, because it's your answers that are correct. Whichever it is, these 12 things have served me well in my negotiations.

1 Process
Negotiation is a process. If you follow it and trust it, you will get a solid result. Everything else is icing on the cake that will help smooth and optimize the process. But remember the five steps and deliver them with commitment, consistency, and diligence: prepare, open, bargain, close, follow-up.

2 Integrity
Personal integrity is at the core of all good negotiations. You need the other party to trust you and having integrity means that their trust will be well placed. Be honest but maybe not completely open.

3 Respect
The person you are negotiating with is not the same as either their position or their behaviour. Their position may seem unreasonable and their behaviour may drive you crazy. Feel free to deprecate either or both. But never stop respecting the person. They are doing the best they can, just as you are. And if you lose your respect for them, the chances of reaching a negotiated agreement will drop like a rock.

4 Preparation
Prepare fully and with care. If you are not prepared, find a way to delay the negotiation until you are. Start with a checklist of everything you need to consider and cover it all before you start negotiating.

5 Know what you want
When you prepare, pay careful and equal attention to your negotiating goal and your best alternative to a negotiated agreement (BATNA). That way, you know what you are aiming for and when to walk away. And, if the negotiation gets close to your BATNA, get ready to fight hard and to walk away if necessary.

6 Open strong

Make a strong first impression and then build rapport. Never start negotiating until you are clear what the ground rules and authorities are.

7 Questions and listening

These two go together. If you want better, clearer answers, ask better, clearer questions. And if you want to understand the other party and calibrate your offers and requests well, listen carefully to what they say.

8 Flexibility

The most flexible party to the negotiation is most likely to bring about success. Search out all the variables, understand their needs, priorities and preferences. Be prepared to make painful concessions because it's the whole deal that counts. Treat individual parts of it as expendable. Then trade diminishing requests and concessions.

9 Summarize

Take notes, record agreements and frequently summarize and confirm where you are. Check everything, take nothing for granted. This way you can build your agreement, step by step, with each one resting on a solid base.

10 Close

Someone has to close to create an agreement. Don't be fearful that you will break rapport. If you stay respectful and represent the position accurately, the relationship will survive a 'no'. And when you have closed, it's time to shut up.

11 Follow-up

Don't throw away all the work you put into negotiating an agreement by being negligent with your follow-up. Make a checklist of things to do and follow it with rigour.

12 Reflection

If you want to get better at negotiating, do it more and review each experience. Examine what happened with honesty. Determine the chains of cause and effect and chance that led to the outcome. Extract insights and lessons that you can apply the next time.

Summary points

- Carry out a team lessons-learned meeting that will allow everyone on your team to reflect on, and learn from, their experience as part of your negotiating team.

- Get into a regular habit of reflecting on your workplace experiences. However, whether you do that or not, always reflect on the experiences you had during a negotiation. That's how you'll get better at it.

- The best review of this book is the one you prepared for yourself. Ignore the author's summary; what matters is what you found interesting and helpful. Why not share it with colleagues in a social media post? It will help them a little bit, and help you a lot, by fixing those important ideas in your own mind. And don't forget to namecheck *How to Negotiate* by Mike Clayton.

Appendix 1
Negotiation preparation checklist

This document should be marked as CONFIDENTIAL and circulation strictly controlled.

Part 1: You

Outcomes

☐ Define your negotiating goals
For example, your ideal terms, target outcomes or the agreements you want to achieve.

☐ Identify secondary goals
These are things that would be nice to achieve but are not essential.

☐ Clarify potential requests that are non-negotiable.

Position

☐ Your real position
This is the least favourable terms you would be willing to accept. You will never disclose this.

☐ Your opening position
This is what you plan to state at the outset of the negotiation, subject to what you learn at the open stage.

☐ Your stated position at various stages as the negotiation progresses

You may role-play or do a scenario analysis to establish possible positions.

☐ Your best alternative to a negotiated agreement (BATNA)
This is what you do if you cannot achieve an agreement.

Self-assessment

☐ Strengths
Your personal (and team) strengths, going into the negotiation.

☐ Weaknesses
Your personal (and team) weaknesses, going into the negotiation. Also assess how you will either compensate for these or ensure they do not become relevant.

☐ Resources
Everything you can draw upon to support you (and your team).

☐ Leverage
The advantages you have, to move the negotiation towards an agreement that favours your objectives.

☐ Flexibility
All the ways you will be able to adapt to prevailing circumstances.

Part 2: The other party

Opposition research

Track record, culture, approaches, values, and behaviours of:

☐ The individual or individuals
☐ The organization

Position

☐ Goals
☐ Needs

☐ Priorities

☐ Preferences

☐ BATNA

Part 3: Context

Evaluate the context for the negotiation

☐ History and past events that are relevant to the negotiation or one of the parties' attitudes.

☐ Cultural, regional or sectoral factors that can affect expectations, priorities or decision-making.

☐ Organizational and regional cultural preferences that can affect etiquette and communication styles.

☐ External pressures and trends that affect both parties, such as regulation, legal obligations, technology change or market conditions.

Part 4: Strategy and plan

Zone of possible agreement (ZOPA)

☐ Determine the likely overlap between your interests and those of the other party.

☐ Anticipate potential areas of agreement and conflict.

☐ Identify requests and concessions you can make that work within the ZOPA.

Plan

☐ Determine your initial negotiating strategy
It could be to negotiate hard, make easy concessions, compromise to get agreement, collaborate for a win-win or walk away.

☐ Identify a representative range of negotiation scenarios
Play them out to determine what you can learn from them that will help build a robust plan (and a contingency plan).

☐ Plan out concessions you will request

☐ Plan out concessions you can offer

☐ Build a negotiating plan
See Appendix 2.

☐ Draft your opening statement
This will contain your opening position. Consider the extent to which this will be an outline at one extreme, or a formal document that you will share, at the other.

☐ Consider what can go wrong and develop a contingency plan for the scenarios that merit one.

Team

☐ Determine the negotiating team roles you will need

☐ Assemble your negotiating team
Some members may fulfil multiple roles.

☐ Assign team roles and brief individuals

☐ Determine processes for team communications and decision-making.

☐ Carry out a team briefing.

Part 5: Logistics

Shared logistics: confirm or organize

☐ Time and date for negotiation

☐ Venue or call for negotiation

- ☐ Meeting room or virtual facilitation, discussion, presentation, and recording tools
- ☐ Agenda

Your own (or team) logistics: confirm or organize

- ☐ Travel arrangements
- ☐ Accommodation and subsistence arrangements
- ☐ Visual aids
- ☐ Ensure all materials, reports, documents and data are accessible and organized
- ☐ Check data security and reinforce procedures

Appendix 2

Negotiation plan template

This document should be marked as CONFIDENTIAL and circulation strictly controlled.

Meeting agenda

Insert meeting agenda here.

Part 1: What we want to achieve

Our goals	
Our interests	
Our BATNA (best alternative to a negotiated agreement)	
Our leverage	

Part 2: Logistics

Meeting location Details of venue or online meeting	
Meeting date and time	
Travel, accommodation and subsistence	

Part 3: Team

Team members and roles	

Part 4: Meeting plan

Overall negotiating strategy/ approach	
Opening position	
Questions to ask	
Key points to make	

Requests to make	
Concessions available to make	
'Red line' concessions not available	
Risks and indications to be aware of	

Other considerations

Appendix 3

Sample negotiation agenda

Objectives	The purpose of this meeting is...

Meeting time	The purpose of this meeting is...
Meeting place	

Attendees	
John	*Role*
Paul	*Role*
George	*Role*
Ringo	*Role*
Diana	*Role*
Florence	*Role*
Mary	*Role*
Barbara	*Role*

Start time:	
1. Welcome and introductions	
2. Agreement of ground rules and authorities	
3. Opening positions/ opening statements	
4. Discussion of opening positions/opening statements	
5. Discussion of issue A	
6. Discussion of issue B	
7. Discussion of issue C	
Break	
8. Discussion of issue D	
9. Discussion of issue E	
10. Discussion of issue F	
11. Summaries and review of discussion so far	
12. Agreement	
13. Plan for follow-up	
Close	

Appendix 4

Agreement follow-up checklist

1. Immediate tasks: completing the agreement admin

- ☐ Document your agreement in writing
- ☐ Circulate your agreement document for comment and confirmation
- ☐ Secure confirmation that the written record of your agreement is a true representation
- ☐ File the document securely

2. You and your team

- ☐ Thank your team (if you have one) for their work
- ☐ Conduct a team lessons-learned review
- ☐ Give individual feedback to team members
- ☐ Reflect on your own performance and note what you learned

3. Actions under the agreement

- ☐ Create a plan to carry out the follow-up tasks
- ☐ Allocate responsibilities to team members (if you have them)
- ☐ Carry out the necessary tasks

☐ Track your performance and that of the partner in your agreement

☐ Issue gentle reminders if needed

4. Managing the relationship

☐ Thank the counterparty for their conduct of the negotiation

☐ Consider whether to offer feedback and do so if appropriate

☐ Nurture the relationship throughout delivery of the agreement

☐ Create regular check-ins to monitor status

5. End of agreement

☐ Confirm the end of the agreement

☐ Review its success in meeting expectations

☐ Carry out team and personal reviews for final lessons learned

☐ Discuss future agreements with your partner

Appendix 5

Negotiating team responsibility matrix

Negotiation Role	Responsible	Contributor	Consulted	Sign-off
Lead negotiator				
Deputy lead negotiator				
Performance coach				
Observer: Reading the room				
Analyst				
Legal adviser				
Technical adviser				
Strategy adviser				

Negotiation Role	Responsible	Contributor	Consulted	Sign-off
Cultural adviser				
Risk manager				
Relationship manager				
Note taker				
Administrator				
Red team				
Ultimate decision-maker				

Appendix 6
Structured framework for a lessons-learned review

1. Opening your meeting

Welcome

You won't need introductions, but do allow some informal time for relationship strengthening.

Recognition

Take some time to recognize and celebrate contributions, successes and exceptional achievements, as a way of setting a positive frame for the meeting. And recognize any special circumstances the team had to contend with.

Purpose of the meeting

This will be around learning and improvement. Also use this to define the outcome you want for the meeting.

Style

Set the tone you want by encouraging people to be open to sharing, to listen respectfully to each other, to avoid assigning blame or making personal criticisms and to participate fully. Focus people's attention on gathering lessons for good practice and performance improvement. This means paying attention to actions and behaviours, rather than people. Ask everyone to keep the meeting positive and highlight a growth mindset whereby we look for ways to incrementally improve. Emphasize that everyone has something to contribute.

2. Discussion and exploration

The first of the two main parts of the meeting is where you will identify and explore the themes for your lessons learned.

Here are some examples of how you can organize your discussion. You can do so by:

- Negotiating stage
- Team role
- The structure of the final agreement
- Events and issues that arose
- Methods, tools and techniques you used

Things to discuss include:

- Objectives and priorities
- Effectiveness of preparation
- Understanding of the negotiating parameters: positions, BATNA, ZOPA
- Choice of negotiation strategy and tactics
- Relationship building, interpersonal communication and reading the room
- Team performance as a team
- Flexibility and response to emerging situations: outcome and relationship
- Success in terms of outcome and relationship

3. Drawing conclusions

In this section you will refine the lessons you identified in the last section and prioritize them so that those with a lesser impact do not distract from the substantial lessons.

Use a consensus approach (such as voting) to prioritize. Then work together to articulate:

- The lessons learned, which can be statements of good practice or recommendations for change
- Actions that flow from the lessons learned
- Responsibilities for follow-up actions
- Implementation time scales, if appropriate
- How you will communicate the lessons learned

4. Closing your meeting

- Reinforce responsibilities for follow-up actions
- Confirm your next steps
- Thank everyone for participating and contributing

Appendix 7

Glossary of negotiating terms and acronyms

80:20 rule: See Pareto Principle.

Anchor: A reference point that influences the choices or decisions a person will make.

Anchoring effect: A subconscious bias that leads people to rely too heavily on an initial piece of information.

BAFO: Best and final offer. The best offer you can make, upon which you will not improve.

BATNA: Best alternative to a negotiated agreement. What you would do if you cannot reach agreement, so it is the point below which a negotiation will not yield an advantageous agreement.

Bottom line: The minimum outcome a negotiator is prepared to accept. Defined by the BATNA.

BPA: Best possible agreement. The best result a negotiator can get from a negotiation.

Broken record approach: Continuing to repeat a request or a response until the other person changes their approach.

Buyer's remorse: The feeling of regret after committing to an agreement. It usually results from a belief that a better agreement was possible.

Buying back the deal: Doing anything after the agreement is made that leads the other party to regret their decision and pull out of the agreement.

CDM: Consensus decision-making. A group decision-making process in which participants work towards a shared agreement on the right decision.

Closing gambit: A tactic used at the close of a negotiation to move the other party towards a final agreement.

Cognitive dissonance: The discomfort we feel when we try to hold two conflicting beliefs at the same time.

Concession: A benefit or compromise that one negotiator offers the other to help move towards an agreement.

Conditional close: A closing gambit where a negotiator suggests one or more conditions upon which they will make an agreement. They invite their counterparty to accept the conditions.

Deadlock: A situation where both parties believe no further progress is possible.

Heads of agreement: The outline of the contract you aim to draft and commit to. Also called heads of terms.

Interests: The needs, priorities and preferences that motivate a negotiator.

ITT: Invitation to tender. A formal document inviting a supplier to offer a formal proposal to meet a buyer's requirements.

JV: Joint venture. A business entity where two or more organizations agree to work together, bound by an agreement but remaining independent of each other.

KYIV analysis: An alternative to MoSCoW analysis for prioritizing options. KYIV stands for Keep for sure; Yes, if we possibly can; If we get the chance, we will; and Very unlikely – don't pursue.

LAA: Least acceptable agreement. The minimum agreement a negotiator is prepared to accept before walking away. Formally, it is when the agreement matches the BATNA, but the negotiator may have an LAA that is better than their BATNA, to avoid the feeling of making a poor agreement.

Leverage: The advantage one party has which allows them to move the negotiation towards an agreement that favours their objectives.

Loss leader: A product or service that is sold at a loss to attract customers and build a commercial relationship that will bring profit in the long term.

M&A: Mergers and acquisitions. Business transactions that involve the joining of companies. Mergers involve the creation of a new organization to hold the assets and activities of the preceding organizations. Acquisitions are the purchase of one business by another, and its incorporation into the structures and operations of the purchaser.

MDO: Most desired outcome. The best result a negotiator could get from the negotiation.

MEEO: Multiple economically equivalent offers. A number of offers or proposals that have the same economic impact (benefit) for the organization receiving the offers. See also MEEP, MESO.

MEEP: Multiple economically equivalent proposals. A number of offers or proposals that have the same economic impact (benefit) for the organization receiving the offers. See also MEEO, MESO.

MESO: Multiple equivalent simultaneous offers. A number of offers or proposals that are made at the same time, and have the same value for the organization receiving the offers. See also MEEO, MEEP.

MLATNA: Most likely alternative to a negotiated agreement (see also BATNA). The most probable result a negotiator would achieve if they walked away from the negotiation.

MoSCoW analysis: A prioritization process that categorizes each alternative into one of four priority ranks: musts, shoulds, coulds or won'ts.

Negotiation: The process of searching for an agreement that satisfies all parties. Alternatively, conflict that follows a process and proceeds in a respectful manner.

Pareto Principle: The observation that, in many circumstances, a large proportion of effects arise from a small number of causes. It is often called the 80:20 rule because of the high frequency of approximately 80 per cent of outcomes being caused by approximately 20 per cent of the causes.

Position: A predetermined solution or end point to the negotiation, or a discussion, that a negotiator adopts.

PEST analysis: A simple approach to identifying trends, pressures or sources of risk from four perspectives: Political, Economic, Social and Technical. See also PESTLE analysis, SPECTRES analysis.

PESTLE analysis: A simple approach to identifying trends, pressures or sources of risk from six perspectives: Political, Economic, Social, Technical, Legal and Environmental. See also PEST analysis, SPECTRES analysis.

Rapport: A sense of understanding one another and feeling a bond.

Reactance: The need we feel to resist and push back against a choice that we perceive someone to be imposing upon us.

Red lines: Things that a negotiator will not compromise on. Fixed positions that the negotiator believes represent vital interests.

Retrospective: A meeting where a negotiating team reflects on its experiences and draws lessons that will improve its performance in a future negotiation.

RFI: Request for information. A formal document that a buyer issues to potential suppliers, asking for information that it can use to assess which ones to invite to submit a formal proposal.

RFP: Request for proposal. A formal document that a buyer issues to potential suppliers, asking for a binding proposal to provide goods or services for stated commercial terms.

RFQ: Request for quotation. A formal document that a buyer issues to potential suppliers, asking for a binding price against a specification for goods or services.

ROU: Record of understanding. A document that sets out the terms that negotiators have reached. It is not legally binding, but serves to ensure mutual understanding.

SME: Subject matter expert. A professional with a high degree of competence in a specific area of knowledge or practice.

Social proof: The influence we feel when other people, with whom we identify, think or act in a certain way.

SWOT analysis: A simple analysis tool that negotiators can use to analyse the Strengths, Weaknesses, Opportunities and Threats of anything – like themselves, the opposition or an option, for example.

SMARTEST goals: An enhanced version of the more familiar SMART goals, tailored to the negotiating context. The acronym stands for: Specific, Meaningful, Ambitious, Realistic, Trimmable, Ethical, Substantiated, Timeframe.

SPECTRES analysis: A simple approach to identifying trends, pressures or sources of risk from eight perspectives: Social, Political, Economic, Commercial, Technological, Regulatory, Environmental and Safety or Security. See also PEST analysis, PESTLE analysis.

Sunk cost trap: A bias where we give too much decision-making weight to what we have already committed, rather than the future commitment and benefit. It can lead to investing more time, effort or money into something that is no longer a sound investment.

Tender: A formal proposal to provide goods or services.

Trial close: A negotiating tactic where one negotiator asks questions of the other to gauge how close they are to being ready to make an agreement.

Walk-away point: The point in a negotiation where a negotiator needs to walk away, because the terms are no longer favourable enough to continue. This is usually where the terms match the value of their BATNA. See also BATNA, MLATNA.

WATNA: Worst alternative to a negotiated agreement. This is the worst possible outcome if the negotiation fails. Useful to understand for risk management. See also BATNA, MLATNA.

Win-win: Informal name for a collaborative negotiation strategy where both parties 'win' or increase the benefit they get by further positive contributions to the potential agreement.

Zero-sum game: A negotiation where here one negotiator's gain is exactly balanced by the other's loss, resulting in a net gain of zero.

ZOPA: Zone of possible agreement. The range of potential agreements where both parties' interests are satisfied. If their interests do not overlap, there is no ZOPA, and a mutually beneficial agreement is not possible.

Appendix 8

Deepen your understanding of negotiation: further reading

I have been highly selective in my recommendations, choosing only 10 books that will really add to your understanding of the ideas in this book. All of them are both highly authoritative and very readable.

General negotiation

Getting to Yes: Negotiating an agreement without giving in, Roger Fisher and William Ury, Random House, 2012

Never Split the Difference: Negotiating as if your life depended on it, Chris Voss and Tahl Raz, Random House, 2017

Psychology

Working with Emotional Intelligence, Daniel Goleman, Bloomsbury Publishing, 1999

Thinking: Fast and Slow, Daniel Kahneman, Penguin, 2012

Spoken communication

*How to Speak So People Listen,** Mike Clayton, Pearson, 2013

Improve Your Communication Skills, Alan Barker, Kogan Page, 2025

Influence

Influence, New and Expanded: The psychology of persuasion, Robert Cialdini, Harper Business, 2021

How to Influence in Any Situation,* Mike Clayton, Pearson, 2015

Body language

What Every Body is Saying, Joe Navarro, Collins 2008

The Book of Tells, Peter Collett, Bantam 2004

* These books are written by the author of *How to Negotiate*

From 4 December 2025 the EU Responsible Person (GPSR) is:
eucomply oÜ, Pärnu mnt. 139b – 14, 11317 Tallinn, Estonia
www.eucompliancepartner.com

www.ingramcontent.com/pod-product-compliance
Lightning Source LLC
Chambersburg PA
CBHW040919210326
41597CB00030B/5126